Heirloom Seeds and Their Keepers

Heirloom Seeds and Their Keepers

Marginality and Memory in the Conservation of
Biological Diversity

• • • • • • • • • • • • • • • • • • •

VIRGINIA D. NAZAREA

• • • • • • • • • • • • • • • • • • •

The University of Arizona Press   Tucson

The University of Arizona Press
© 2005 Arizona Board of Regents
All rights reserved
∞ This book is printed on acid-free, archival-quality paper.
Manufactured in the United States of America

10 09 08 07 06 05   6 5 4 3 2 1

Library of Congress Cataloging-in-Publication Data

Nazarea, Virginia D. (Virginia Dimasuay), 1954–
Heirloom seeds and their keepers : marginality and memory in the
conservation of biological diversity / Virginia D. Nazarea.
p. cm.
Includes bibliographical references (p.   ) and index.
ISBN 0-8165-2435-1 (cloth : alk. paper)
1. Seeds. 2. Germplasm resources, Plant—Collection and preservation.
3. Traditional farming. 4. Agrobiodiversity conservation. I. Title.
SB117.N189 2005

                                        2004026290

CONTENTS

Figures

Table

Preface

• • • • • • • • • • • • • • • • • • • •

Difference and disorder dance, like fireflies, all around us. Some of us delight in the display of light, others wish to tame the disturbing lack of any perceptible pattern, while still others, taking fireflies for mosquitoes (or realizing the difference but dismissing it as irrelevant), seek to erase the source of their discomfort and annoyance. Most of us vacillate between these sentiments.

So, too, our relation with the diversity and complexity on earth takes on many forms, often shuffling back and forth between these forms as we negotiate our individual and collective predilections and juggle various aspects of our beings. A wetland, a lawn, an urban center, a biological corridor, or a tangled plot of beans and greens provokes memories and equations, attachment and detachment, endorsement and condemnation, hope and despair, and hardly from clear or fixed decision-making criteria or matrices.

What makes seedsavers—and by this term I mean the independent gardeners and small-scale farmers who save and pass along folk or "old-timey" varieties without any formal organization or design—special is the place they hold for diversity in their hearts and in their fields. What *makes* a seedsaver is a kind of marginality characterized by engagement rather than remoteness, by joyful irreverence rather than outright resistance, by celebration rather than protest, and by creative openings rather than dead-end walls. In the face of spreading global monocultures, seedsavers find their place or make one.

My interest in biodiversity has come nearly full circle with this book. *Cultural Memory and Biodiversity* (University of Arizona Press, 1998) was about the role of multiple and fuzzy decision-making criteria and pockets of memories at the margins in the persistence of the diversity of sweet potatoes despite the onslaught of market integration and agricultural extension. My main concern was how the diversity of knowledge and practices of sweet potato farmers buttresses the genetic diversity of this crop in the face of development and commercialization. Here, I am more concerned with the proclivities and idiosyncrasies of gardeners and farmers who are continuing to cultivate a wide array of edible, medicinal, and ornamental plants in their plots. My focus is not just on how cultural memory serves as a means to conserve biodiversity but also on how biodiversity, embodied in plants that sprout with great abandon, evokes sensory recall and releases us from the spell of organized forgetting. I wonder about the connection between seedsavers' "uncaptured" minds and their "undisciplined" landscapes and marvel about their elaboration of a very touching and compelling counter to homogenization of fields and spirits engendered by modernity.

I take the position that seedsaver contribution to the conservation of biodiversity needs to be understood as conservation *in vivo*, or conservation as a way of life. It cannot be "idiomed" away as haphazard management or sustainability by default. Nor can it be straightened, ordered, and tidied up for wider and more efficient application. To appreciate it fully and to learn its lessons, we have to be open to a different set of epistemology, meaning, and valuation—a looser framework that may pave the way for a humbler science; one that admits fluidity and complexity, even quirkiness. And learn the lessons *we must* as we wean ourselves from the historically colonial appropriation of plant genetic resources in botanical gardens and gene banks to a more enlightened position of facilitating conservation in situ and in partnership with small-scale farmers and old-timey gardeners who have been quietly conserving biodiversity for generations in their fields.

With their heirloom plants, seedsavers embroider the landscape with memories that awaken connections to past and place in many of us. Through an informal network of exchange, ritual, and celebration, they embellish a countermemory that helps us dig in rather than fade out. And, by giving us some reassurance that we are not alone, they enjoin us to explore a realm of possibility instead of surrendering to a discourse of loss. Faced with an ethnographic difficulty of foregrounding that which derives its power from its marginality, I have decided to go all the way in paying tribute to these farmers and gardeners by using their actual names as well as the names of the plants they cherish and hold in place for all of us. I thank them all for their contribution and for this privilege.

For support in fieldwork and writing, I gratefully acknowledge the funding agencies of the research projects included in this work. These are the Ford Foundation and the International Rice Research Institute for supporting my research on agricultural decision making of rice farmers in Laguna, Philippines; the User's Perspective with Agricultural Research and Development and the International Potato Center (CIP) for the memory banking research on sweet potato diversity in Bukidnon, the Philippines; the U.S. Department of Agriculture's (USDA) Sustainable Agriculture and Research and Education Program for the Southern Seed Legacy Project; the U.S. Agency for International Development's Sustainable Agricultural and Natural Research Collaborative Support Program (SANREM CRSP) for ethnoecology and biodiversity research in Nanegal and Cotacachi, Ecuador; and the U.S. Department of Agriculture's Agricultural Research Service for the Vietnamese Introduced Germplasm Project. My appreciation goes to Gordon Prain of CIP and Henry Shands of the USDA for invitations to meetings that started me thinking about these issues, and to Carlos Perez of SANREM CRSP for generous support of my research and publications.

Most of the research projects from which I draw material for this book were collaborative undertakings, although the stream of consciousness is mainly mine. When writing in the first person plural, I am referring to my intellectual partnership with Robert Rhoades and acknowledging our students and "memory bankers" who have helped document these seeds and memories: Maricel Piniero, Eleanor Tison, Lan Jia, Katy Price, Sandra Crismon, Kathy Couch, Hieu Tran, Shiloh Moates, and Juana Camacho. Much as I would like to claim the credit, without their dedication and active participation, there would be no story to tell. Maricel and Kathy, and at various stages, Juana, Milan Shrestha, and my daughter, Natasha Sandoval, have also helped me through the processing of this text, patiently putting up with my own fuzziness and technology marginality. The Anthropology Department at the University of Georgia has supported me in my quest to finish this book. Thanks to the department head, Michael Olien, and the staff: La Bau Bryan, Margie Floyd, Arnold Brunson, Charlotte Blume, Stephanie Kollman, and Jill Morris. They have seen me through floods and outages, with a lot of cheer to spare.

With deep appreciation and affection, I dedicate this book to my colleague, best friend, and husband (not in any particular order), Robert Rhoades, who dusted off, and lovingly bound together, all my loose chapters.

Heirloom Seeds and Their Keepers

CHAPTER 1

It Takes a Village Clown

. . . .

Glory be to God for dappled things—
For skies of couple-color as a brinded cow
For rose-moles in all stipple upon trout that swim
All things counter, original, spare, strange—
Whatever is fickle, freckled (who knows what?)
With swift, slow; sweet, sour; adazzle, dim;
Praise him.

—Gerard Manley Hopkins, *Pied Beauty*

There is a rich diversity of ways to think about biodiversity. Characterized as "variety or multiformity, a condition of being different in character and quality" (Patrick 1997:1), and used to describe "the variety of
life forms, the ecological roles they perform, and the genetic diversity
they contain" (Wilcox 1984:71), biodiversity can be measured at different levels (genetic, species, and ecosystem) and viewed from many different angles (past fragmentation, present erosion, and future use). The
term *biodiversity* was coined as recently as 1986 when the National Fo-
rum on BioDiversity was organized by the National Academy of Sciences and the Smithsonian Institution in Washington, D.C. By 1992, it
had captured enough attention to become a household word as well as a
rallying point in the Rio Earth Summit (Wilson 1997). Credited with a
wide range of direct uses—food, medicine, fabrics, dyes, construction
materials, ritual essentials, and raw materials for industry, plant breeding,

and biotechnology—along with critical environmental services, including maintenance of nutrient and hydrologic cycles, regulation of air quality and water purity, preservation of habitat, and reservoir for evolutionary change (Daily 1997; Chapin et al. 2000; Beattie and Ehrlich 2001), biodiversity is arguably the mandala of the 1980s and 1990s. It continues to unfold and still shows no sign of disappearing from scientific and public imagination and concern today. In the opening paragraph of the landmark volume *Biodiversity*, E. O. Wilson (1988:3) declared:

> Biological diversity must be treated more seriously as a global resource, to be indexed, used, and above all, preserved. Three circumstances conspire to give this matter an unprecedented urgency. . . . exploding human populations are degrading the environment at an accelerating rate. . . . science is discovering new uses for biological diversity in ways that can relieve both human suffering and environmental destruction. . . . (and) much of the diversity is being lost through extinction caused by the destruction of natural habitats. . . . Overall, we are locked into a race. We must hurry to acquire the knowledge on which a wise policy of conservation and development can be based for centuries to come.

The urgency of biodiversity conservation is not simply an alarmist call to create mass hysteria or a charismatic lure to generate more funding or sell books, as some would claim. Unparalleled population growth and rates of consumption, which in turn drive habitat destruction and fragmentation, introduction of exotic species, global climate change, and overharvesting and commercialization of the earth's resources, contribute to the crisis of extinction and genetic erosion (Myers 1996; Patrick 1997; Lovejoy 1997). The dominance of economic considerations over ethical-ecological ones only exacerbate these vulnerabilities (Ehrlich 1988; Norgaard 1988). At the rate that biodiversity is being decimated— according to Peter Raven and Jeffrey McNeely (1998:13), "the natural wealth of our planet is being lost at an estimated rate of 5 percent per decade"—there is real reason for concern.

Since the mid-1990s, scholarly critiques have been formulated regarding the twin ideas of "biodiversity" and "biodiversity conservation."

That biodiversity is, more than anything, a social/political construct (Takacs 1996; Ribiero 1997) and "a historically produced discourse" (Escobar 1998:54) that needs to be problematized is *good to think about*— as, I might add, are other constructs like nature, development, equity, and gender. Yet this does not diminish the gravity of the environmental consequences and cultural repercussions of these constructs. Deeper understanding of the problem certainly requires theorizing beyond the obvious and the absolute to penetrate created realities and demand for solutions, but at some point pressing issues must be confronted. The threat of genetic erosion cannot be ignored; it is just as good to think about and more than that, *good to do something about*. Despite its bumper sticker aplomb, "erosion is real, extinction is permanent" is a mantra that is not too far off the mark.

Several developments have precipitated a call to action: (1) the growing list of endangered species; (2) the increasing scientific recognition of the need to conserve the underlying ecological processes supporting biological diversity; (3) the realization that biodiversity occurs at multiple spatial scales and levels of organization; and (4) the widening acceptance that systematic conservation strategies are more effective than the ad hoc single-species approach of the past (Groves et al. 2002). In terms of crop genetic resources, the Food and Agriculture Organization estimates a rate of disappearance of 1–2 percent per annum, from which the Rural Advancement Foundation International (RAFI) infers that we may already have lost close to 75 percent of agricultural biodiversity (RAFI 1997). In short, there is growing consensus that biodiversity loss is accelerating and irreversible, its consequences unfortunately dire. Without a doubt, there is an urgent need for an integrated scientific, ethical, and policy response. That being said, the main argument of this book is that we must indeed hurry or we could lose the race. Yet, we should not be in so much of a hurry to beat the "wolf at the door" that we forget the complex nature of interactions and gloss over the nuances of biodiversity conservation on the ground.

One aspect of biodiversity in particular bears closer inspection from the perspective of anthropology and public policy because it is linked inextricably with human culture and management, so closely in fact that

Figure 1 Polyculture (photo by Kathy Crouch)

biological and cultural diversity define and create each other and ultimately merge. Such is the case of the cultivation of agricultural crops at various scales, including horticultural interest in polyculture (fig. 1) as opposed to monoculture (fig. 2). This can go in two directions in relation to biodiversity conservation. One direction, more often discussed and bigger in scale, is the narrowing of the genetic base of cultivated plants or declining agrobiodiversity. The trend toward genetic uniformity has been particularly dramatic for staple and commercial crops. Since World War II, for example, nearly all of the local wheat varieties in Greece, Italy, and Cyprus, the indigenous sorghum races of South Africa, and the older varieties of brussel sprouts have been abandoned, usually upon the introduction of high-performance hybrids (Plucknett, Smith, Williams, and Anishetty 1987). Dramatic increases in yield as well as national and international support for modern varieties of crops have all but banished landraces, or traditional varieties, from farmers' fields, making agrobiodiversity more critical in many respects than the "natural" biodiversity

Figure 2   Monoculture (photo by Maricel Piniero)

that exists in the wild. In contrast, in small-scale farming or subsistence production, including what are referred to as dooryard gardens, backyard gardens, or home gardens, diversity is generated, enhanced, relished, and protected at every turn, ensuring its persistence and making uniformity untenable (Stoler 1978; Fernandes and Nair 1986; Padoch and de Jong 1991; Lamont et al. 1999). These marginal spaces deserve thoughtful reexamination as natural and social scientists, environmental conservationists, and development practitioners grapple with the erosion of the genetic diversity of crops and their wild relatives along with the attrition of cultural knowledge pertaining to these plants (Hawkes 1991; Brush 1991; Alcorn and Oldfield 1991; Soleri and Cleveland 1993; Holden et al. 1993; Nazarea 1998).

In the past, ritual, seasonality, and commensality in foodways and lifeways contained, but at the same time reinforced, variability, flux, and idiosyncrasy. To a certain extent, this seeming contradiction continues to fuel biodiversity conservation but more so at the margins of market-driven production systems. What goes on at the margins subverts integration and homogenization but, for mostly the same reasons, it also eludes macroanalysis of causal factors and resultant trends. Hence, the contribution of the margins tends to go unacknowledged. I suggest that to understand this vitality, it is worthwhile to look beyond the "best farmer" and his "model farm" and search instead for the village prophet, or the village clown. In this book, the village clown stands for irreverent strategies or "marginalities of the mind" that serve as a potent antidote to the sweeping monoculturization of fields and spirits.

In mainstream agriculture, the push toward homogeneity embodied in monoculture and commercialization is quite powerful, and oftentimes irresistible. Landraces or folk varieties of crops are rapidly displaced, becoming obsolete or archaic as new varieties are bred or engineered and aggressively promoted through various agricultural programs backed up by extension and credit infrastructures. These infrastructures do not just provide positive support that enables farmers to "get on the train" of modernization but actually possess built-in deterrents to nonadoption such as crop insurance or farm loans predicated on adoption of modern cultivars and technology packages. The history and hype of the Green Revolution is replete with discoveries of high-yielding "miracle varieties," which, supported by a package of technological "magic bullets," can alleviate hunger and poverty in the Third World. The second coming, or the age of biotechnology, promises even more productivity and constructs a more colorful, if scary, landscape of "golden rice," "Roundup-ready soybeans," and "terminator genes." The cultural dynamic behind this problematic trend was aptly described by Vandana Shiva in *Monocultures of the Mind* (1993:12):

> The fragmented linearity of the dominant knowledge disrupts the integration between systems. Local knowledge slips through the cracks of fragmentation. It is eclipsed along with the world to which it relates. Dominant scientific knowledge thus breeds a monoculture of the mind by making space for local alternatives disappear, very much like monocultures of introduced plant varieties leading to the displacement and destruction of local diversity. Dominant knowledge also destroys the very *conditions* for alternatives to exist, very much like the introduction of monocultures destroying the very conditions for diverse species to exist.

The obliteration of alternatives concomitant with the narrowing of the genetic and cultural base of cultivated plants brings with it a significant loss of resilience of previously diverse agroecosystems. In many parts of the so-called Third World, the introduction of "best," "miracle," or "elite" varieties of rice, corn, wheat, potatoes, and other staple and secondary crops may have increased production in some well-endowed areas, but it has wrought havoc on the diversity and stability of these agroecosystems, in both sociocultural and biological terms (Fowler and Mooney 1990; Brush 1992; Altieri 1999).[1] Let us consider, for a moment, the changes that have occurred from the time of small-scale, low-input farming dependent on saved seeds of traditional varieties of crops to large-scale, input-intensive agribusiness dependent on hybrid or genetically engineered seeds. Gary Nabhan, in *Enduring Seeds* (1989), wrote about traditional farmers whose "relative resilience" has contributed to the creation and maintenance of an environment stable enough for locally adapted crop varieties to flourish. He went on to describe the legacy of these farmers:

> Locally adapted cultivated plants are variously referred to as folk varieties, land races, heirloom vegetables, crop ecotypes, or *razas criollas*. They represent distinctive plant populations, adapted over centuries to specific microclimates and soils. They have been selected also to fit certain ethnic agricultural conditions: the field designs, densities, and crop mixes in which they have been consistently grown. Aesthetic selection has also taken place, as the taste, color, and culinary preferences of a particular culture have favored the forms and chemical characters of some plants over others (73).

In the course of agricultural research and development, however, the range of "forms and characters" became drastically restricted as delight and fancy regarding various tastes, colors, textures, and aromas were replaced by what Jack Harlan, a prominent plant breeder and collector, called a "pure line mentality." According to Harlan (1972:212):

> A pure line mentality, convinced that variation was bad, uniformity was good, and off-types in the field somehow immoral, developed.

Symptoms of the mental climate could be found in crop judging
contests, ribbons awarded at county and state fairs, seed certifying
agencies, and in some state and federal seed acts. It did not seem to
occur to anyone that a deliberate mixture of cultivars could be a
useful alternative to pure line culture.

Notice how, in this abbreviated history, changes in human cognitive and
cultural frameworks have driven the conservation, or erosion, of crop
diversity. The increasing dominance of the pure line mentality with respect to agricultural crops and the perceived immorality of variation in
the field culminated in an extreme paradox, as people came to regard the
fertile, resilient seed as "primitive and raw germplasm" and the sterile,
input-dependent hybrid seed as the "finished product" (Shiva 1993).
From this kind of logic, it followed that what was primitive and raw
needed to be modernized, and quickly (fig. 3).

Largely due to the hegemony of agricultural commercialization, farmers' options are increasingly restricted to input-sensitive "elite" varieties
and the technological packages on which they are dependent.[2] In many
developing nations, this trend is approaching a point of reification wherein
the existence of alternatives is hardly recognized, creating, overall, a potent and debilitating form of cognitive sclerosis. In the Philippine low-
lands, for instance, only farmers in their sixties or older know anything
about the cultivation and use of traditional rice varieties because younger
farmers were successfully wooed and weaned on the Green Revolution
formula of modern, high-input monoculture in the 1960s and 1970s. So
pervasive is this mind-set that the "Green Revolution generation," that
is, farmers presently in their fifties, are wont to emphasize control and
commercial potential over harmony and beauty in their indicators of
sustainability and quality of life (Nazarea et al. 1998). Contrast this with
a practice that Harold Conklin observed in the 1950s among the
Hanunoo in Mindoro, the Philippines, of reserving a special plot near
the house that is used exclusively for collecting new or unfamiliar cultigens "of great horticultural interest" (1957:110). This plot was distinguished from the general category of slash-and-burn field, or swidden,
and farmers added to it with every interesting discovery. Potential use or

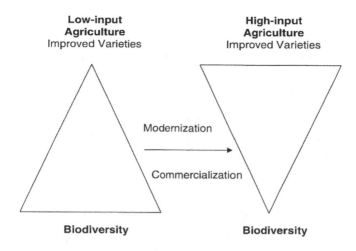

Low-input
Agriculture
Improved Varieties

High-input
Agriculture
Improved Varieties

Modernization

Commercialization

Biodiversity   Biodiversity

Figure 3 Inverse relationship between modern, improved varieties and biodiversity

benefit may have been a motivating factor for the Hanunoo, but wonder and delight at things that looked, smelled, or felt different must also have played a major part.

With each passing generation, and with tightening market integration, cultural knowledge will likely shrivel in proportion to the phasing out of folk varieties or landraces in favor of modern ones. This can be carried to extremes as agricultural science follows medical science in its search for wide-spectrum antibiotics and attempts to design the crop variety for all seasons and all reasons. For instance, one goal of international rice research is to breed or engineer the "ideotype," or the ideal variety, along with a prescribed set of cultural management practices (Khush 1996). The rice ideotype is characterized by an even more reduced and compact vegetative structure and longer, heavier panicles than the high-yielding dwarf varieties of the Green Revolution, thus further minimizing lodging and maximizing productivity (fig. 4). For as long as cultural and scientific devotion to monocultures and ideotypes hold sway, one can only speculate to what extent and at what pace the associated

TRADITIONAL   IMPROVED

IDEAL

Figure 4 Traditional, improved, and ideotype varieties of rice (Source: Peter White, "Rice: The Essential Harvest," *National Geographic* [May 1996])

local knowledge will wither away. A lack of alternatives—actual or perceived—predisposes local people to ever-increasing homogenization and dependency, and loss of memory.

Cultural memory is relevant to the conservation of biodiversity because it counters the sometimes overwhelming pull to surrender all options to external, prepackaged solutions. Much of conventional development discourse is characterized by the prevalence of the viewpoint that we must "disappear" the old, the archaic, to make way for the new, or the "politics of disappearance" (Shiva 1993). This has engendered not just a loss of pride but an actual sense of shame, a plight not restricted to developing countries. Wendell Berry was speaking of rural America when he wrote:

As the local community decays along with local economy, a vast amnesia settles over the countryside. As exposed and disregarded soil departs with the rain, so local knowledge and local memory move away to cities or are forgotten under the influence of homogenized sales talk, entertainment, and education. The loss of local memory and local knowledge—that is, of local culture—has been ignored, written off as one of the cheaper "prices of progress," or made the business of folklorists. (1990:157)

Given this rather dismal scenario, it is important to note that the nested structure of multiple cores and peripheries nevertheless constitutes a confounding complexity that allows for the hidden life of *multiple and shifting margins*. At the margins flourish pockets of memories and resistant tendencies that allow alternatives to proliferate, resulting in the persistence of both cultural and genetic diversity (Nazarea 1998). Recently, the term *countermemory* has been proposed to foreground memory that stands in opposition to official narratives of the past, thereby challenging its hegemony (Lipsitz 1991; Stoller 1995; Zerubavel 1995). Likewise, at the margins, a form of countermemory embodied in diverse fields and home gardens—as well as in senses and emotions—stands in opposition to the hegemony of monoculture. In ways similar to natural ecotones and geographical or cultural borders, where dominance and stasis are held at bay by competition and equitability, marginal spaces allow *room for play* and enable what James Scott referred to as everyday forms of resistance, or resistance of the weak (1985).[3] I should hasten to add that while the concept of everyday resistance is valid and useful here, the "resistors" themselves are often unaware that they are resisting anything, or that they are weak, and therein lies a different kind of power and strength. As an insightful and disarmingly candid informant from the Southern United States once remarked to me, "Until they told me I was poor, I thought I was doing quite alright!"

Sherry Ortner (1995:174–75) noted that, "Once upon a time, resistance was a relatively unambiguous category, half of the seemingly simple binary, domination versus resistance. Domination was a relatively fixed and institutionalized form of power; resistance was essentially organized opposition to power institutionalized in this way." She points out, however,

that, in tandem, the attention drawn by Foucault to "less institutionalized, more pervasive, and more everyday forms of power" and the analysis by Scott that emphasized the "less organized, more pervasive, everyday forms of resistance" resulted in the breakdown of this binary. We
are now left to deal with the psychological ambiguities and conflicts as
well as the sociopolitical complexity of resistance. Are there cases, for
example, wherein resistance is not so much a matter of "foot dragging"
(Scott 1985:xvi) as digging in? Here is where I think marginality offers
an inviting playground. Marginality provides cracks and crevices that
make it possible for the less integrated to improvise and hold their own;
in some cases with the result of opening the cracks wider (Nazarea-
Sandoval 1995). Sense of place is bivalent and, with respect to being marginal, "in my place" can be both inhibiting and liberating. I would argue
that the resilience, expediency, and fuzziness of decision-making frameworks and coping strategies of small-scale farmers and gardeners are effective as countermemory, or counterhegemony, precisely because they
are ad hoc and sheltered at the margins of modern, commercial agriculture, where they can carve out a more sovereign space (fig. 5).

Western and non-Western literary traditions alike, as well as popular forms of entertainment, are almost universally spiced with the "Chal-
lenger" or "Transgressor" of generally held beliefs and unquestioned
assumptions. In folk stories worldwide, the burdens and insults of daily
life are lightened by the funny, willful, and crafty character known as the
Trickster. The Trickster comes across as "the creatively antinomian over-
reacher transgressing the artificial codes of society and the categories of
human perception that give rise to these codes. . . . Trickster's violative
behavior places him at the margin or even beyond the social pale: from
such a vantage point he liberates humans from conventional social moral
boundaries and dramatizes new ways of perceiving and the possibility of
new orders" (Ballinger 1989:15). In other words, the proverbial Trickster
provides the "'tolerated margin of mess' necessary to explore alternatives
to the present system and to contemplate change" (Babcock 1985:185).
Simply by being, the Trickster entices us to abandon fear and predictability and embrace possibilities.

Significantly, heightened perceptiveness and cunning are always

Figure 5 Bukidnon woman selecting favored sweet potato varieties for home consumption (photo by Maricel Piniero)

bestowed by storytellers, who are themselves marginal, on the less powerful, as exemplified by the "Tar Baby" in its many reiterations. Tracing parallels and connections between trickster tales in the Southern United States with those from West African storytelling traditions, Patricia Jackson-Jones observed:

> Both cultures delight in imbuing physically insignificant and seemingly helpless creatures with extra-ordinary mental acumen. Their superior intelligence and discretion make these small beings not only godlike in powers but models for much stronger creatures to emulate. The "helpless" animal may take the form of the spider of the Slave Coast, the rabbit of the Sierra Leone region, or the *blakanyana* of South Africa. . . . Regardless of the region, these animals are heroic figures in the same tradition of Brer Rabbit in Gullah and inland

black literature, or Ananse the spider in Caribbean literature. . . .
Seldom does one find massive or ferocious animals like the lion, the
leopard, the elephant . . . depicted as shrewd and insightful. They
are continuously portrayed as stupid and perpetually duped by smaller
animals who must from necessity live by their wits, not from their
strength (1987:111–13).

A sense of delicious danger comes from the tension of an insider-
outsider vantage point, for while the Trickster is a member of the social
circle, it is perpetually thinking and operating "outside the frame." Yet it
knows the workings of the system well, as only an insider can. As Kimberly Blaeser (1995:51) pointed out in a compendium of North American trickster tales, "Ambiguity approaches truth in a way that clarity
cannot." We can say in the same way that the margins, with all their
playfulness, insubordination, and elusiveness, approach truth in a way
that the center cannot. Trickster tales are steeped in ambivalence, disorder, and alterity in every culture included here and in others (Nazarea
and Guitarra 2004). My objective in this book is to illuminate seedsaver
gardens as repositories of ambiguities and alternatives that can effectively counteract homogenization and avert cultural and genetic erosion.

The Transgressor who takes liberties with rigid social norms has
taken many forms. In nineteenth-century England, gypsies and tinkers
were referred to as "masterless men," reflecting the powerlessness of
state policy against vagrancy, and were targeted—for the most part un-
successfully—for spiritual "reclamation" by evangelical Protestant missionaries (Helleiner 1995). Filmmaker Federico Fellini regarded clowns
as, on one hand, "solemn and authoritarian" yet, on the other, "the first
and most ancient anti-establishment figures" and considered it "a pity
that they are destined to disappear under the feet of technological
progress" (Stoddart 2000). In A History of the Circus, George Speaight
pointed out that "clowns in a circus supply a necessary element of anarchic
foolery to balance the discipline of the acrobats and the obedience of
animals. Where everything else is neat and controlled, they are wild and
unpredictable" (1980:96–97). Without proposing an exact equivalence,
I wish to carefully explore these threads of resistance, marginality, and

nonchalance, for they may help explain that certain "condition of being different in quality and character" possessed by small-scale farmers, heirloom gardeners, and seedsavers that accounts for their distinct and significant contribution to the persistence of biodiversity. Such an understanding may help identify ways to cultivate, rather than repress, this creative force.

This book highlights the contribution of farmers and gardeners who save, propagate, and pass on folk varieties or heirloom seeds to the conservation of biodiversity. My coworkers and I have encountered these farmers and gardeners in the context of several research projects that I will discuss in chapters 3, 4, and 5. What has impressed me most about them is how, like the proverbial Trickster or village clown, they stand out because of the ambiguities and the "tolerated margin of mess" that their form of agriculture and the resulting diversity of their fields force us to acknowledge. This peculiar character, evidenced by their tangled plots and their dotted landscapes, seems to tease and taunt the hegemony of agriculture across geographical, cultural, and political borders. Theirs is *conservation as a way of life*, or *conservation without design* as we know it. Whether found in the developed or the developing world, these hardy and self-possessed individuals successfully resist the vortex of agricultural homogenization and challenge the inevitability of increasing uniformity and simplification. Scott (1985), who examined the degree to which hegemony is imposed by "elite homilies," concluded that although ideology may be successful, for the most part, in making things appear as inevitable, it stops short of passing things off as legitimate and unchangeable. Unimpressed and uncaptivated, the margins represent a countervailing force, and take exception to what Arturo Escobar (1995:53) referred to as the "coherence of effects that the development discourse achieved . . . the discursive homogenization which entails the erasure of complexity and diversity."

While sympathetic to critiques of development, I tend to be skeptical of what strikes me as the solemnity of antidevelopment discourse because such gravity denies the hard-to-ignore spontaneity and irreverence of everyday habits of ordinary actors. As a "halfie" anthropologist myself (Abu-Lughod 1986), with one foot planted in my native soil and one foot wedged in the Western academic door, I have witnessed far too many instances of local field assistants and informants who gleefully provide visiting anthropologists with all sorts of ghost stories or plant lore that they wish to hear, traditional chieftains and healers mocking outsiders who get carried away with their rituals, and women who find the dominant positionings of men hopelessly pompous and endlessly amusing—among themselves and all in secret of course. Mary Margaret Steedly referred to these instances as "'unofficial' accounts of personal experience that move against the grain of the official discourses in which they are embedded. Always susceptible to official absorption or exclusion, these histories nevertheless have a certain power of their own, which is the subversive power of partiality, the power of the singular event to confound explanation" (1993: 238). Steedly's point resonates and haunts when one reflects, on the one hand, on national and global programs for biodiversity conservation that either downplay or attempt to homogenize local initiatives and successes and, on the other, on antienvironmentalism rhetoric that denies the ingenuity and perceptiveness of local people by making them out to be mere victims, copies, and/or mouthpieces of outside experts.

Hypercoherence, in the end, is illusory and overblown; victimization only superficially a one-way street. Neither cogs in the functioning of the ecosystem or of social movements nor pawns in the development or conservation game—at least in the absolute sense—recalcitrant seedsavers invent their own beat and chart their own directions, in interesting and delightful ways. Thus, they are not burdened by the rebel's ire but rather moved by a searching, creative spirit. They are not outsiders, although oftentimes they behave as if they were. They not only demonstrate their uncanny knowledge of social boundaries but also constantly stretch and test these limits. From my perspective, the role of seedsavers should be examined more closely for its critical significance in deterring wholesale surrender and loss of cultural memory and genetic diversity; in other words, in countering the homogenization that development imposes. Such rethinking, I believe, demands a new conceptual framework, one that offers an alternative to the macrostructural study of large-scale forces (and discourses) that shape development and conservation.

When the Marginal Is Central

In "Anthropology and the Conservation of Biodiversity," Benjamin Orlove and Stephen Brush (1996) discussed the increasing contribution of anthropologists, from the 1970s up to the present, to the study of human impact on the world's plant genetic resources. They emphasized the centrality of human cognition, decision making, and behavior to biodiversity conservation and reviewed anthropological perspectives on the problem under four themes: the ethnobiology of agricultural diversity, the cultural ecology of plant genetic resources, participatory conservation, and the politics of genetic resources. Asserting that anthropological investigation should focus on the persistence of diverse farming systems under changing conditions such as population growth or cultural change, Orlove and Brush pointed out that "the challenge is to avoid essentializing the stewardship of biological resources as ecological nobility or the processes of change as misguided technology adoption. Ethnobiologists must be attentive to the complexity of plant populations in dynamic and patchy social contexts" (1996:342). They further recommended that anthropologists pay attention to the conservation of biodiversity at different spatial, social, and political scales that link local populations, national agencies, and international organizations. With reference to the politics of genetic resources, in particular to intellectual property rights and farmers' rights, the authors declared that "the lack of economic valuation for genetic resources managed by farmers means that they have no incentive to conserve them" (1996:344).

To be truly "attentive to the complexity of plant populations in dynamic and patchy social contexts," as suggested by Orlove and Brush, I think we must shift some of our attention from conceptual, aggregate units such as "organizations" and "populations" (whether local or not) to actual people—*people* who acquire and pass on knowledge collectively and individually, who not only participate, organize, and make decisions

but also experiment and hedge, make-believe and play. We need to trail
our gaze from the center to the margins, from the significant to the mundane. I believe we should face the new imperatives in plant genetic resources research and conservation not with comfortable old habits but
with new visions and directions, however tentative and partial. To continue to dwell on significant events at the center will only reentrench the
notion of passive farmers and gardeners at the mercy of development
and reinforce the power of outside agencies over their fate as well as the
fate of the plants they cultivate. Ironically, pursuing new visions and
directions may necessitate refurbishing our ethnographic toolkit and
generating "thick descriptions" of text and context. Anthropologists, in
particular, need to highlight the embodiment of a conservation ethic at
the margins, one that does not necessarily fall into line with the streamlined, rapid appraisal mode common in interdisciplinary research as well
as with interventionist programs percolating from the top.

The complexity of biodiversity conservation, particularly its cultural
dimension, requires less monolithic frameworks and formulaic approaches
than we have employed in the past. It would also help if we acknowledge
what many of us have suspected all along: Economic valuation for genetic resources managed by farmers is a logical antidote to the skewed
distribution of rewards in the global marketplace, but it may not be the
sole, or even the most compelling and enduring, incentive for farmers to
conserve diversity. We need to recognize in farmers greater perceptiveness and agency than we have, as a rule, given them credit for and start
thinking of them as actors in their fields, not just as participants in "participatory programs" that we are supposed to help design and imple-
ment. In terms of the management of plant genetic resources at the local
level, the inertia is most likely toward the conservation of biodiversity
because of the multiplicity of farmers' evaluation criteria, the patchy and
dynamic environment in which they operate, and the resulting flexibility
of their decision making.

In an insightful discussion of farmers' responses to homogenization,
A. R. Vasavi (1994) related how the farmers of Bijapur, in South India,
used to manage their agricultural operations guided by the precepts of
bhumi-guna (quality of the land), *hada* (appropriateness), and *hulige*

(abundance). From their exposure to the Green Revolution that swept the Indian countryside in the 1960s and 1970s, however, they have been conditioned to think and become *sistam*, connoting uniformity and compliance with strict rules aimed solely at maximizing production. As described by Vasavi (1994:293):

> So pervasive is the sense of a need to change, and to be different from what they are now, that village residents have incorporated the rhetoric of being systematic, of being sistam, into their vocabulary. Often used as a reference point, village residents refer to the need to be sistam, and show appreciation for things that are sistam. Homes of educated persons are sistam, urban people are more sistam than they are themselves, and grooms from urban and educated homes will bring sistam to their wives.

And yet many of these same people refer, tongue in cheek, to the present as *hibred kala* (hybrid times), and to themselves as *hibred mandi* (hybrid people), and liken themselves to the hybrid seeds that they now sow— "weak, delicate, dependent, and susceptible to diseases" (1994:283). Akhil Gupta (1998) was discussing hybridities, too, but with respect to epistemologies and practices of agriculture, when he argued that the farmers of Alipur "neither fit the mold of indigenous people who have been uncontaminated by modernity nor that of progressive farmers on the brink of entering the takeoff stage of capitalist development. As such, they render ambivalent narratives of progress and modernity embedded in postcolonial discourses of development" (1998:157). It seems that the farmers of Bijapur and Alipur internalize and reflect the dominant development ethos, but at the same time they twist it round and round, this way and that, trying to penetrate and question its many facets.

Writing about postcolonial development in a similar vein with reference to South Africa, John and Jean Comaroff argued:

> Conquered and colonized societies were never simply made over into the European image, despite the persistent tendency of Eurocentric scholars to speak as if they were. Rather, their citizens struggled, in diverse ways and with varying degrees of success, to

deploy, deform, and diffuse imperial institutions. What's more, the
colonizers themselves were transformed in the process, often in
unexpected ways. Thus, new political systems were born from count-
less couplings of 'local' and 'global' worlds, from intersecting histories that refocused European values and intentions thus rerouting,
if not reversing, the march of modernity. (1993: xii)

The contradictions and ambivalence inherent in modernity confound
neat before-and-after comparisons and binary oppositions, as the
Comaroffs emphasized. They also expose the problematic foundation of
the concept of local people's (or women's) "empowerment" so popular
in development and conservation circles. Imputing directionality while
at the same time establishing a certain inviolable hierarchy of goodwill,
empowerment subtly imposes its own form of authority, and of surrender—
the well-dressed end product of the double task of emancipation and
subordination. Where does power reside and who, after all, is vested to
endow power on another?

On the northern Colombian Pacific Coast, Afro-Colombian women
continuously craft their own expression of autonomy and creativity in
the form of raised gardens, or *zoteas*. Zoteas are typically old wooden
canoes supported by mangrove stilts that contain a great variety of medicinal, aromatic, "power," and edible plants as well as condiments and
spices indispensable for cultural continuity and social exchange (Camacho
2001). The women enrich the soil in their zoteas by adding humus,
sand, ashes, and ant soil and also use them as nurseries for germinating
seeds of fruit trees collected from the forest (fig. 6). The seedlings are
then transplanted to the *fincas*, or farmers' fields, in effect linking the
domestic space with larger agricultural and natural spaces. Descendants
of African slaves who were introduced in the region to work in gold and
silver mines during the colonial period, these Afro-Colombians have in-
dependently and creatively synthesized a combination of soils, water,
and biodiversity into a concoction of culturally valued species richness
that is close to the house and protected from marauding animals and
treacherous floods.

According to Juana Camacho (2001:37), "Zotea management is

considered a woman's domain. It begins in early childhood in the family land and is consolidated when a woman signals her adult status by marrying, having a child, and establishing a garden of her own." She quotes a popular local saying, "A woman is like a zotea. . . . a zotea has two legs, a body, and the plants which are dress, because a zotea without anything is like a naked woman" (2001:35). This saying is more illuminating than any economic equation or conservation design in explaining why the zotea continues to be a marginal but persistent repository of cultural memory and genetic diversity that is indispensable to women's agency in the Pacific Choco bioregion. It reminds us that identification from within is more important than empowerment from without.

The foregoing discussion indicates that human cognitive and emotive predispositions play a major part in engineering shifts in dominant management strategies regarding plant genetic resources. In the same manner that cultural appreciation of various colors, tastes, textures, and aromas moves gardeners and farmers to conserve a diverse array of folk varieties or landraces, the cultural depreciation of diversity through standardization leads to the precariously narrow genetic base of modern varieties and ideotypes. Even conservation biologists are beginning to recognize the pivotal role that the social sciences can and must play in turning things around. As Paul Ehrlich pointed out:

> Thus, what is desperately needed now is a much better understanding of the ways in which culture evolves and determines most interesting human behavior, including humanity's treatment of its life support systems. We need to comprehend how cultural evolution produces the vast diversity of human natures—different fundamental attitudes, beliefs, proclivities, preferences (in the economic sense), and behaviors (Ehrlich 2000). That should help discover how to reconfigure social, political, and economic incentives and cut through barriers of ignorance and denial, allowing society to turn to a path toward sustainability. Some of the most important products of human cultural evolution are ethical concerns, including concerns for nonhuman organisms and environment in general. . . . The job of social scientists is daunting, since the interactions among the elements of

Figure 6   Afro-Colombian *zotea* (photo by Carlos Tapia)

culture rival in complexity those of the global ecosystem of which humanity is an increasingly dominant component. (2002:32)

In our research on the interconnections between cultural and genetic diversity in more peripheral production systems in southern Luzon and southern Philippines, Southern United States, and South America, my coworkers and I have encountered individual acts of resistance and irreverence to the hegemony of mainstream agriculture that conspire to keep the "inevitable" from happening.[4] Farmers and gardeners who collect, exchange, and plant seeds that are saved from year to year by kin, friends, and neighbors have managed to hold off agricultural commercialization at arm's length and to hold on to varieties and practices that are meaningful in their own particular contexts. Like scientists working in gene banks, these independent seedsavers are plant collectors and curators in their own right, although at a smaller scale than we are used to thinking. Their "gene banks" are their home gardens and farms; they have informal networks in lieu of professional organizations. For them, seeds represent memory and identity, not simply accessions for cataloguing or raw materials for plant breeding or genetic engineering. Generally hidden in the shadows, but almost universally present wherever there is a patch of land to cultivate, they expand humanity's pool of options simply by being there; in other words, more as a matter of consequence rather than of intention.

Behind Every Gene in the Field

Historically, one problem that has persistently confounded Western thought is, in a law-governed, supposedly predictable universe, What is the seemingly inexhaustible source of "radical novelty?" Ilya Prigogine (1997) referred to this problem as the "Epicurus dilemma," after the Greek philosopher who first expressed consternation at how, if the world consisted of atoms falling down through the void at the same rate and on parallel paths, novelty associated with combinations of atoms can ever be imaginable. Along the same lines, we can ask, why does informal seedsaving and exchange persist despite the efficiency, profitability, and sheer convenience of more modern seed sources and agricultural practices? Moreover, given the strong pull of standardization and uniformity, why do seedsavers continue to delight us and confuse us with their fanciful and seemingly irrational devotion to admixtures of edible, medicinal, and ornamental plants? In other words, what is behind the persistence of diverse combinations of genes in fields and gardens in the context of homogenizing agricultural and cognitive monocultures?

Recently, in a brave and novel declaration, Hjorleifur Jonsson described games by the Mein, an ethnic minority in Thailand, and demonstrated the vitality of minority cultural dynamics and resistance in the context of national integration. On the premise that "Fun needs to be taken seriously. This does not involve taking the fun out of it," he argued that these performances constituted a critical political play and were not any less effective in countering integration because they were fun. In fact, he concluded, "The fun of the fair and related events concerned issues of class, gender, ethnicity, administrative recognition, official attentions, sexuality, and threats of violence. While fun and play may be irreducible and irrepressible and thus best left as such, ethnography can benefit from attention to how agency, identity, and social reality are entangled in the serious play and fun of everyday life" (2001:169). In the spirit of "serious fun" and "anarchic foolery," I submit that a better understanding of the role and contribution of seedsavers can come from airing out our ponderous paradigms and admitting elements of fascination, surprise, and joy. The conservation of local alternatives can come from two metaphors—the metaphors of *jumping genes* and *colporteurs*. It is my belief that these metaphors capture the contingency and serendipity of conservation in real life, or at the ground level. To ignore the special nature of unplanned and unstructured conservation in farmers' fields and gardeners' plots is to gloss over their most significant contribution and to risk harming it in the zeal to systematize, institutionalize, and globalize our efforts.

In the next chapter, I will attempt to weave these metaphors together in the hope of shedding some light on significant, albeit at times tangential, conservation of plant genetic resources that goes on at the margins, without design, yet quite effectively. In chapters 3 to 5, I ground these metaphors on the ordinary lives of farmers and gardeners based on our past and ongoing research on local knowledge and plant genetic resources conservation. Chapter 3 provides an overview of various research projects and the characters that made them interesting. It also details the early part of this research trajectory, focusing on local knowledge, memories, and decision making of small-scale rice and sweet potato farmers in the Philippines. In chapter 4, I present the life histories of some farmers and gardeners around the American South who participated in the Southern Seed Legacy, a continuing research and action project aimed at conservation and transmission of heirloom seeds and associated cultural knowledge. Chapter 5 explores a new dimension of seeds for "rooting" and reterritorialization, or as sources of identity, reconstruction of the homeland, and conduit of intergenerational connection in an adopted, often persistently alien, landscape by discussing some results of our current researches,

"Introduced Germplasm from Vietnam: Documentation, Acquisition, and Implementation" and "Ethnoecology of Fragile Lands in the Andes."

In chapter 6, having analyzed some common threads in the life histories of these individuals, I contrast their everyday motivations and practices with the institutional discourse and framework for biodiversity conservation at national and global levels. Here, I examine efforts by local, small-scale farmers to conserve and enhance their plant genetic resources and compare these to global institutional programs that tend to purge key attributes of on-the-ground conservation. I also question the notion that conservation has to be "by design," to be accomplished mainly through integration and intervention. Finally, in the concluding chapter, I take a second look at marginality and resistance in relation to the generation of diversity, both cultural and biological. I try to demonstrate how research on this problem might profit from a confluence of exciting intellectual developments in anthropology and other disciplines and point to some possible directions for productively melding conservation by design with conservation as a way of life.

In sum, then, my intention in this book is to explore a road, not necessarily less taken but certainly less recognized, in the conservation of biodiversity and the emerging research concentration, "anthropology of biodiversity conservation." It departs from the analysis of trends, extraction of rules, and implementation of designs and instead concentrates on the meaning and contribution of ordinary lives, sensory stimuli, and countermemory to the conservation of biodiversity. Emphasizing the role for the social sciences in general and for anthropology in particular, it is intended not so much as a critique but rather as a complement to existing frameworks for on-farm or on-site (in situ) conservation of biodiversity; one that strives to bring a human face to "farmer decision making," "farmer selection criteria," and "formal and informal seed flows." As Cary Fowler, Geoffrey Hawtin, and Toby Hodgkin remarked in the foreword to *Genes in the Field* (Brush 2000), "Appreciating the significance and value of something that has been present for so long is never an entirely comfortable or smooth process. Terminology—and the encrusted notions it sometimes hides—is challenged straightaway."

If we think about it, the nurturance of biodiversity in farmers' fields has existed for as long as farmers have cultivated, and tinkered with, their plants, whether driven by scarcity and need or curiosity and fun. For this reason, we need to be cognizant of, and faithful to, the mechanisms and dynamics that have favored the persistence of genes and gene complexes in home gardens and small-scale farms as well as at the borders of commercial plots. It boils down to what Janice Alcorn, speaking as discussant in a Society for Applied Anthropology session entitled "Local-Global (Dis)Articulations in Plant Genetic Resources Conservation" in Washington, D.C., in 1996 (see also Rhoades and Nazarea 1999), referred to as "conservation with a small c" to distinguish it from major global initiatives, or "conservation with a big C." I proceed by presenting two intriguing and, in my view, relevant metaphors—the first from genetics and the second from philosophy and history. Both, I hope, will pave the way for a better appreciation of the complex web of memories, longings, gardens, kitchens, and palates behind every conserved gene in the field.

A Tale of Two Metaphors
Jumping Genes and Colporteurs

• •

Every biologist surely recognizes that some useful characters did not arise by selection for their current roles: why have we not honored that knowledge with a name? Does our failure to do so simply underscore the unimportance of the subject? Or might this absent term, in Foucault's sense, reflect a conceptual structure that excluded it?
—Stephen Jay Gould and Elisabeth Vrba, "Exaptation—A Missing Term in the Science of Form"

Of course, oppression is damaging, yet the ability of social beings to weave alternative, and sometimes brilliantly creative, forms of coherence across the damages is one of the heartening aspects of human subjectivity.
—Sherry Ortner, "Resistance and the Problem of Ethnographic Refusal"

This tale is born of two disparate genres. From two genres come two metaphors, both deviating from a central tenet in Western thought—linearity. In genetics, the axiom of linearity is embedded in the physical structure of the chromosome on which are lined particulate, and quite independent, hereditary units called genes. In history and philosophy, linearity is expressed as directionality and predictability of historical time, Fernand Braudel's *longue durrée* (1980). Progress is seen from this perspective as a continuum of refinement and achievement, with modernity at its pinnacle, of the rest catching up with the West. This mind-set is contagious for, as George Lakoff and Mark Johnson pointed out, "our ordinary conceptual system, in terms of which we both think and act, is fundamentally metaphorical in nature" (1980:3). It follows that "the most fundamental values in a culture will be coherent with the meta-phorical structure of the most fundamental concepts in the culture" (1980:22).

Consider the metaphorical structure of the Western conception of time—the past is behind us ("don't cry over spilt milk"), live in the present and use each moment wisely ("time is money"), the future beckons ("the dawning of tomorrow")—and how it privileges or condemns certain activities and lifestyles as worthwhile or wasted. The "metaphors we live by" shape our understanding and structure the way we approach problems surrounding biodiversity erosion and conservation. A shift in metaphors might allow another way of seeing, even perhaps open an-other pathway to action. As Lakoff and Johnson further noted:

> The concepts that govern our thoughts are not just matters of the intellect. They also govern our everyday functioning, down to the most mundane details. Our concepts structure what we perceive, how we get around in the world, how we relate to other people. Our conceptual system thus plays a central role in defining our everyday realities. If we are right in suggesting that our conceptual system is largely metaphorical, then the way we think, what we experience, and what we do everyday is a matter of metaphor. (1980:3)

Cast in a broader framework, metaphor, like memory, can serve as a cultural vehicle that carries with it crucial premises and associations about the world (Lambek and Antze 1996). These suppositions are tenacious and powerful—any counter to them is initially viewed as nothing short of heretical—but they can and do change, as evidenced by the radical conceptual shifts with regards to gene action and historical time that were stimulated by the works of Barbara McClintock and Ernest Bloch. These intellectual developments are totally unrelated to each other except that both have, in their respective fields, shaken assumptions of linearity and predictability in a very big way. The action of jumping genes and the habits of colporteurs infuse our understanding of the phenomena with an appreciation of elements of surprise and serendipity, not to mention great reserves of energy. These elements are critical but slippery and hence often glossed over in research and policy-addressing issues related to biodiversity.

I believe these conceptual metaphors, if applied to seedsaving and small-scale farming and gardening, will help us grasp conservation with a small c, or as a way of life, and at the same time appreciate a slightly different dimension of resistance from the margins. Even if they come up short, these metaphors can still open up a space for reflection and dialogue and hold the place until more appropriate or instructive ones are elaborated. One thing about metaphors is that, like guilt, they keep on giving. This was elegantly expressed by Ann Game and Andrew Metcalfe:

> Whereas literal knowledge aspires to the inert status of information, *metaphor works with indeterminacy to keep meaning safe from final clarification that is its obituary.* Meaning's play is not a game watched over from the outside but one in which we live and through which we understand. We may fantasize about mastering literal knowledge, fixing it in our memories or reference books or filing cabinets, but metaphors in knowledges cannot be processed, always maintaining reserves of wisdom beyond our present understanding . . . the meaning of rich metaphors keeps blooming; people think further by growing into them, awakening to their implications. . . . We do not come empty-handed to our performances and metaphors. When metaphor engages us, we respond through the emotions and memories that reverberate with the role. (1996:50–51, emphasis added)

Initiatives in biodiversity conservation can now be said to be emerging from the Dark Ages and entering an Age of Enlightenment (see chapter 6). The emphasis has shifted from remedial biological conservation of targeted endangered (or, alternatively, charismatic) species to a more proactive and integrated management of ecological relationships and patterns of diversity at multiple scales. Local knowledge and landraces are being recognized as not only important but quite indispensable to the conservation of plant genetic resources. Likewise, the crucial role of indigenous peoples, subsistence farmers, and women in the conservation of plant genetic resources is increasingly acknowledged and factored into current research and development agenda. Finally, on-site or in situ conservation in protected areas and farmers' fields is being promoted as a viable complement to ex situ conservation in distant botanical gardens and scientifically managed gene banks. These are undoubtedly significant, commendable strides. However, despite these new initiatives that have reshaped scientific paradigms and institutional mandates, there remains a disturbing rigidity, linearity, and normativeness in current approaches that to my mind contradicts the articulated position of recognizing local conservation and to some extent violates the very nature of that contribution. Witness, for instance, the jarring juxtaposition of two incommensurate worlds: On the one hand is heirloom (or traditional, folk, old-timey) gardening, chaotic and evocative; on the other is scientific, on-farm conservation, ordered and systematic. These two worlds can meld—and biodiversity conservation can draw on their respective strengths—but this melding cannot be based on the denial of difference or on the assumption of superiority of one over the other.

Transposable Lessons from Barbara McClintock

In the 1940s, the pioneering studies of Barbara McClintock, a geneticist and plant breeder at the Carnegie Institution of Washington's Department of Genetics in Cold Spring Harbor, New York, challenged the dominant paradigm that genes were fixed, linear entities in the genome. She demonstrated in corn that there were certain genes—transposable elements or "jumping genes"—that could move from one position to another in the chromosome and "leap" between chromosomes in response to environmental stresses that threaten the genome. According to McClintock (1984:792):

> There are "shocks" that a genome must face repeatedly and for which it is prepared to respond in a programmed manner. . . . Some sensing mechanism must be present in these instances to alert the cell to imminent danger, and to set in motion the orderly sequence of events

that will mitigate this danger. But there are also responses of genomes to unanticipated challenges that are not so precisely programmed. The genome is unprepared for these shocks. Nevertheless, they are sensed and the genome responds in a discernible but
initially unforeseen manner.

Noting the turbulence in genetic activity whenever the cell is faced with
serious stress, she started pursuing the search for "how a genome may
reorganize itself when faced with a difficulty for which it is unprepared"
(1984:793). McClintock's discovery came barely two decades after the
rediscovery of the principles of genetics so painstakingly outlined by an
Austrian monk in the 1800s. Experimenting with peas in the sanctuary
of the monastery, Gregor Mendel had formulated the laws of genetics
that governed the inheritance of discrete, independent traits. McClintock's
research was first published outside of Cold Spring Harbor annual reports as a brief account entitled, "The Origin and Behavior of Mutable
Loci of Maize" in the *Proceedings of the National Academy of Science* in 1950.
Later, she presented at the prestigious Cold Spring Harbor Symposium
and received a reaction from her colleagues that can only be characterized as skeptical to hostile. She did not try again until five years had
passed, and even then her presentation was greeted with a lukewarm
reception (Keller 1983; Comfort 2001). Like that of Mendel's before
her, McClintock's pathbreaking work was well before its time and, as a
result, nearly slipped into oblivion. By the early 1970s, however, molecular biology began accumulating evidence that not only confirmed the
existence of jumping genes but proved that such was widespread, span-
ning the living world from corn to *Escherichia coli* to mammals. From here
on, it was only a matter of time before the scientific community accepted
that transposable elements are dynamic components of virtually all genomes and can exert significant effects on gene expression and, ultimately,
evolution. McClintock won the Nobel Prize in Genetics in 1983.

Aside from discovering genes that shift and jump, which could easily have been dismissed as a mere oddity, McClintock pointed out that
transposable elements have the ability to create genomic diversity through
chromosome breakage and rearrangement and by altering patterns of
gene expression. She also called attention to how, by serving as agents of

gene restructuring, these elements increase genetic diversity and thereby enhance the adaptive capability of organisms, at times bringing about significant macroevolutionary changes (McDonald 1990). In a speech published in *Science* after she received the Nobel Prize, she challenged biologists to study how the cell "senses unusual and unexpected events and responds to them . . . how the cell senses danger and instigates responses that are truly remarkable" (McClintock 1984). While not all biologists have been convinced of the direct adaptive advantage of transposable elements, many are willing to recognize that even assuming that transposable elements are not features directly favored by natural selection to increase fitness, "this large pool of *nonaptations* must be the wellspring and reservoir of most evolutionary flexibility" (Gould and Vrba 1983:13, emphasis added).

The difference between the action of transposable elements and regular (stable) mutation, of course, is that cells have evolved mechanisms such as splicing and deletion to detect and censor would-be mutations, not to mention the selective disadvantages and outright lethal consequences of deleterious mutations. In contrast, the innocuous jumping genes create genomic diversity by inserting an intricate set of regulatory or processing signals into another gene, or by flanking genes and thereby altering patterns of gene expression through inversions, deletions, and unexpected recombinations. In a review of the discovery and subsequent research on transposable elements, Nina Fedoroff (1984:97–98) concluded:

> The ubiquity of transposable elements and the growing awareness that they are major agents of genetic instability force one to consider their importance in the genetic choreography underlying development and their role in the long-term process of genetic change called evolution. . . . It is as if transposable elements can amplify a small disturbance, turning it into a genetic earthquake. Perhaps such genetic turbulence is an important source of genetic variability, the raw materials from which natural selection can sift what is useful for the species.

Even more interestingly, recent studies examining the genetic sequences of normal plant genes have revealed the presence of miniature inverted-repeat transposable elements (MITES) in and flanking over 150 plant genes. MITES alter gene expression by modifying critical domains of regulatory proteins. These tiny transposable elements may have found a niche in plant genes precisely because their features make them compatible with normal gene expression. Their compactness and normal quiescence make it unlikely for them to significantly affect splicing efficiency (Bureau and Wessler 1994; Wessler 1997). Moreover, MITES are most likely to insert and blend into regions where they are hardly detectable, hence allowing these elements to persist uncensored. These traits are so engaging and out of the ordinary that they have earned for MITE families the names "Tourist," "Stowaway," "Alien," "Heartbreaker," and "Harbinger" (Zhang, Arbuckle, and Wessler 2000; and Wessler 2001) from biological scientists whose own stringent disciplinary selection did not favor whimsical prose. Very recently, active MITES in the rice genome that are believed to have hastened the adaptation of *Oryza japonica* from their tropical range to more temperate regions were discovered and named "mPing" and "Pong" (Jiang et al. 2003; Kikuchi et al. 2003). Overall, the MITES' short size and remarkable sequence variety coupled with their "user-friendly" features make them uniquely suited to insert new regulatory motifs at or near cells and to generate diversity in "a myriad of ways" (Wessler 2001:149).

The groundbreaking scientific investigations of McClintock, Wessler, and other scientists who have researched transposable elements have demonstrated that, first of all, even essentially neutral and deceptively trivial elements can enhance the adaptive capability of cells and thereby increase evolutionary potential. Second, it is precisely because of the noninvasive, nonthreatening nature of the transposable elements' effect on the genome that they evade censure or eviction. Third, these elements can exist in a quiescent state until their activity is triggered by serious biotic and abiotic stresses for which the cell has no preprogrammed response, at which point they introduce interesting chaos in the genome. Finally, while natural selection establishes gene frequencies that are adaptive given the prevailing set of environmental conditions, transposable elements maintain a reserve of flexibility that does not require a generational turnover and thus can effectively override natural selection and enhance chances for survival of the species in critical times. With the use of increasingly sophisticated analytical methods, geneticists are discovering highly repetitive and, on the surface, superfluous DNA sequences derived from transposable elements. Once considered as "junk DNA," these DNA segments have come to be regarded as key to the continuation of life in a changing environment. Reflecting on the growing body of evidence regarding the preponderance of these elements in genomes of eukaryotic cells in organisms ranging from *Aribidopsis thaliana* to *Drosophila melanogaster* to *Homo sapiens*, Feschotte and Wessler (2001: 8923) pointed out that "more and more, genomes are beginning to resemble the family attic where the relics and mementos of several lifetimes are stored and await discovery."

How is this relevant to the conservation of biodiversity by gardeners and farmers at the margins of commercial agriculture? I would argue that seedsaving gardeners and farmers, like jumping genes, insert alternative motifs that pose quiet but nonetheless effective challenges to mainstream agricultural systems. Themselves noninvasive and nonthreatening, seedsavers persist, for the most part unmolested by the powerful forces they so successfully subvert. Upon closer examination, this is not very different—at the sociopolitical level—from Scott's (1985) "everyday forms of resistance" that constitute the only real "weapons of the weak." The analysis gets "curiouser" as we note, following Scott, that revolutions (like mutations) do not comprise the ultimate, or even the most reliable, challenge to the dominant structure because revolutions, by virtue of their visibility, are frequently and powerfully squashed; either that or the rebels quickly take on the character of the deposed. Rather, the real challenge emanates from small but cumulative acts of noncompliance and defiance. In the case of peasants, Scott points to the all-too-familiar instances of foot-dragging, pilferage, and gossip. The case of seedsavers is slightly different, the most important elements being not anger and discontent that lead to false compliance but rather curiosity and daring that lead to joyful self-expression and connection with others. To my mind, this is congruent with Gould and Vrba's (1983) concept of nonaptations, which represents potential flexibility when and if the context of selection changes.

While seedsavers are not aggressive revolutionaries or fiery radicals out to dismantle a power structure or prove a point—unless, of course, celebration can be considered as a novel form of revolution—they nonetheless make significant contributions to the conservation of biodiversity. As I hope to demonstrate, it is in their stillness and tranquility, and in the solace and connection that their gardens provide, that they derive their own empowerment and persistence and secure ours. Their unpredictable gardens and tangled plots comprise an evolutionary "keeping room"—quite harmless, to some maybe even somewhat inane, yet extremely potent. Their alternative landscapes open up unexplored vantage points and provide promising channels for personal and collective transformation. Before we go any further in this discussion, however, we must turn our attention to a political minuet of a different sort—the "discordant notes" posed by colporteurs.

Colporteurs as Purveyors of Resistance

Globalization and modernity assault us on a day-to-day basis, dulling our senses, suppressing our natural gag reflex, and habituating us to what Nadia Seremetakis (1994:8) has called "an epoch of tastelessness." Much of the imposition of modernity, in general, and agricultural development, in particular, is anchored on the "discourse of loss" (Seremetakis 1994:ix), a concept akin to Shiva's "politics of disappearance" (1993:5). The disappearance or effacement of memory is a violence instigated through the power of suggestion on the dominated, or the periphery. This power of suggestion can reasonably be expected to be an all-consuming force for, as Bernard Cohn reminds us in the opening paragraph of *Colonialism and Its Forms of Knowledge*, "The theater of power is managed by specialists (priests and ritual preceptors, historians and bards, artists and artisans) who maintained the various forms of knowledge required" (1996:3). The knowledge specialists can assume many forms and guises but, in the end, this "officializing" strategy creates a pliant, permeable fabric that can then be colored and configured at will. Paul Connerton, writing in *How Societies Remember*, also pointed out that:

The more total the aspirations of a new regime, the more imperi-
ously will it seek to introduce *an era of forced forgetting*. . . . All totalitarianisms behave in this way: the mental enslavement of the sub-
jects of a totalitarian regime begins *when their memories are taken away*.
When a large power wants to deprive a small country of its national
consciousness, it uses the method of organized forgetting. . . . What
is horrifying about a totalitarian regime is not only the violation of
human dignity but the fear that there may remain nobody who could
ever again bear witness to the past. (1989:12–14, emphasis added)

In the present time, ideological battles are rarely as crass or unequivocal as totalitarianism or imperialism. "Isms" have gone out of vogue (most,
in any case, have been banished to the never-never land of political in-
correctness) and, having ceased to command any attention, respect, or
fear, have insidiously metamorphosed into more subtle and seductive
messages occurring at many different levels. Subliminal and insistent,
these messages are powerful in blanketing memory, coercing conformity,
and eliminating a sense of any real alternatives, worth, or agency. In the
mainstream of commercial agriculture, this has resulted in input-dependent monoculture, an inherently unstable production system that relies
on the large-scale cultivation of one main cash crop. In ecological terms,
monoculture channels photosynthetic energy into net primary productivity, typically not of the whole plant biomass but more narrowly into
the production of harvestable, edible, and/or marketable plant parts. This
undeniably anthropocentric selection is accomplished through a strategy of extreme simplification of the crop-based ecosystem by eliminating all possible competitors, including all other plants (usually lumped
together as "weeds") and all insects and other arthropods (decried en
masse as "pests"), and supplementing the system with huge importa-
tions of energy subsidies in the form of inorganic fertilizers, herbicides,
and pesticides. In cultural terms, it displaces local knowledge with external, "scientific" expertise as a guiding principle for agriculture and deval-
ues commensal and ritual practices that require a wide variety of plants
and animals for their persistence. So incongruous, unsatisfying, and de-
stabilizing is this oversimplification of nature and culture that it must,

to borrow somewhat liberally from McClintock, instigate some kind of response that is "truly remarkable."

Just as a shock of some level of significance to the cell may activate transposable elements to generate genomic diversity, the historical repression of memory triggers its own set of countervailing forces. Like McClintock, but from a very different time, place, and perspective, Ernst Bloch (1988 a and b, 1991) refused to be fixated on linearity. As a philosopher of Jewish descent raised and educated in prewar Germany, Bloch rebelled against the ossification of middle-class values and the pretensions of bourgeois liberalism. In his writings, which spanned two continents and influenced European and American intellectuals from the 1930s to the 1960s, Bloch used elliptical symbolism "to induce estrangement from the familiar . . . [and] to provoke his readers to break away from whatever prevented them from becoming conscious of what they were missing, of things they would have to define for themselves" (Zipes 1988:xii). Bloch (1991) noted that spheres of discordant experience randomly punctuate the illusion of normative linearity and continuity of historical time. These "discordant notes" challenge the metanarrative of unidirectionality and predictability. Thus, against the backdrop of modernity portraying itself as natural climax, emptying memory of its contents, and dictating the future in the guise of progress, Bloch articulated the concept of *colportage*.

Colportage refers to the cheap reading materials sold by itinerant booksellers or *colporteurs* of the seventeenth through the nineteenth centuries. Colporteurs peddled bibles, cookbooks, primers, medical books, and, notably, romances, fairy tales, and adventure books—materials that made the oppressive demands and tedious routines more bearable by providing a much-needed escape for lower classes (fig. 7). The term, French in origin, comes from a basket or pack that the popular booksellers typically carried around their necks (Brewer 1898). Unlike their contemporaries, the Italian mountebanks (believed to be the antecedents of the itinerant medicine men), who mounted on their "banks" or benches to entertain and beguile the public in order to sell their potions (Brewer 1898; Henke 1997), colporteurs were rarely viewed as con artists and charlatans. In nineteenth-century France, colporteurs were in

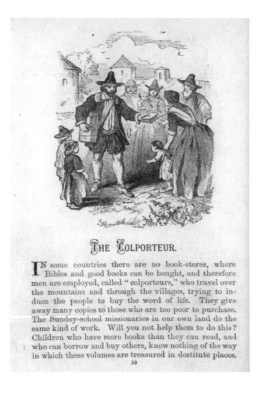

THE COLPORTEUR.

IN some countries there are no book-stores, where
Bibles and good books can be bought, and therefore
men are employed, called "colporteurs," who travel over
the mountains and through the villages, trying to induce the people to buy the word of life. They give
away many copies to those who are too poor to purchase.
The Sunday-school missionaries in our own land do the
same kind of work. Will you not help them to do this?
Children who have more books than they can read, and
who can borrow and buy others, know nothing of the way
in which these volumes are treasured in destitute places.
50

Figure 7 *The Colporteur*, artist
unknown (Source: *New Book
of Two Hundred Pictures*,
American Sunday School
Union, 1868. Courtesy of the
Straight Ahead Pictures
Collection, http://
www.disabilitymuseum.org/
lib/stills/27.htm)

fact highly regarded as "press peddlers" who, by bringing reading materials expeditiously to the masses, were instrumental in evading the con-
trolling French censors. In "The Failings of Popular News Censorship
in Nineteenth-Century France," Thomas J. Cragin reported:

> An 1823 letter from the Paris police prefect demanded that stronger
> measure be taken to control colporteurs, since they spread dangerous
> ideas among the lower classes. Because peddlers could circumvent the
> restrictions placed upon printers and booksellers by obtaining banned
> literature outside of France or in the provinces, the *ordonnance de la
> Prefecture de police* of 21 May 1983 required Parisian peddlers to be
> licensed. These peddlers had to reside in the city for at least one
> year to qualify for a license. The police then issued the colporteur a
> stamped paper license and a *plaque de cuivre*—a medal of the trade
> that bore the labels "crieur" or "afficheur," their authorization, and

their name. Peddlers had to wear the medal around their necks at all times, easing surveillance and enforcement of the law. (2001:61)

The role of colporteurs, however, was not always so serious, or threatening. For the most part, they were considered quite harmless and entertaining and left alone to peddle their books to people who had no access to, or interest in, what could be considered as more mainstream literature. As the fictional character from *Putnam's Monthly Magazine of American Literature, Science and Art* (1854), "Claude the Colporteur," described his offerings:

> *Aubrey*, by the author of *Two Old Mens' Tales*, somewhat loose in texture and extravagant in conception, but powerful and exciting; the story turning upon the love of two twin brothers for the same lady; the one a reserved, studious, and intelligent man, and the other a frank sailor, and ending, of course, in the success and punishment of the subtlest not the best of the two suitors . . . *Nanette and her Lovers*, by Talbot Gwynne, . . . is a story of French domestic life during the era of the revolution. The heroine, at the time it opens, is on the eve of marriage with a young countryman, but the ceremonies are interrupted by a mob. The lover is carried off to join the army, rises in rank, but grows selfish and vain as he rises, and when he comes back, is indifferent to his betrothed, who subsequently marries another.

Bloch, although considered a prominent philosopher of Marxist humanism, refused to dismiss these reading materials for the masses as reactionary because he believed that they assuaged the "hunger of the imagination" of people whose wants he felt must be respected (Zipes 1988). While some of his contemporaries regarded colportage as a form of sedation in that it lulled human consciousness and desensitized it to its own oppression, Bloch perceptively noted that "there is a raw, yet honest substitute for a revolution here, but where else can it express itself but in colportage?" (Bloch 1991:184). He elaborated further—and I think this is what makes the colporteur metaphor particularly relevant to seedsaving and to biodiversity conservation—that "the fairy tale moved on its own in time," nurturing a "wish landscape" that can ultimately lead to a congealment of the "not-yet-conscious" or the "yet-to-become" (Bloch 1988a). In a paper entitled "Better Castles in the Sky at the County Fair and Circus, in Fairy Tales and Colportage," Bloch (1988b:168) wrote, "Toward dusk may be the best time to tell stories. Indifferent proximity disappears: a remote realm that appears to be better and closer approaches. Once upon a time: this means in fairy tale manner not only the past but also a more colorful and easier somewhere else. . . . Fairy tales always end in gold."

Thus, while for the mountebank, the "prime objective was to keep the audience interested but uncritical" (McNamara 1995:3), for the colporteur it was to keep the audience interested *and* critical, as well as—and this is important—hopeful. Hope, in this sense, is the only available recourse from a feeling of inevitability and despair, and a passport to an entire other vision of how things could be. As Bloch argued, "Even well-founded hope can be disappointed; otherwise it would not be hope. In fact, hope never guarantees anything. It can only be daring and point to possibilities that will in part depend on chance for their improvement. Thus, hope can be frustrated and thwarted, but out of that frustration and disappointment it can only learn to estimate the tendencies of countervailing processes" (cited in Zipes 1988:xxv). In this regard, we can think of seedsavers as sowing seeds of hope and bringing us right along with them in their quest for an alternative landscape that is yet to happen. Bloch must also have been referring to hope embedded in colportage when he wrote in his characteristic elliptical style:

> Here, missing meanings are fresh, everywhere, and those that are missing are waiting, as in the fairy tale. The happy ending is fought for and won. Nothing remains of the dragon except the chains. The treasure hunter finds his dream money. The separated lovers are reunited. The fairy-tale-like colportage is like a castle in the sky par excellence, but one in good air, and insofar as this can at all be true about plain wish-work: the castle in the sky is right (1988a: 185).

Focusing on the value of sensory memory and perceptual recall, Seremetakis extended Bloch's notion of colporteurs to include the rural grandmother of a city-dwelling grandchild, the journeyman, the gypsy, the carnival performer, the drunk. These figures, according to Seremetakis (1994:32–33), create a "traffic of exotica . . . ornamenting the everyday with the sensibility of the different . . . forming fragments and animating broken-up pieces of multiple realities in transit . . . bringing to life an alternative world of memory [that is] set up against the structure of repression and displacement called modernity." This countermemory enlivens sensory and cognitive pathways long buried or long lost. Hence, the role of colporteurs is both complicit and constitutive. They provide what Connerton (1989:13) referred to as a "heady release" from forced amnesia, from the hegemony of blahs that most of us tolerate most of the time. To the extent that they are culturally lodged and perceptually salient, they can provoke a questioning of the most deeply entrenched suppositions—a fundamental questioning that may ultimately inspire social movements. For while social movements can be precipitated by a build-up of a sense of injustice and moral outrage (Moore 1978; see also Edelman 2001 for recent review), I believe they are just as frequently and strongly stimulated by a release from reified boundaries and natural-ized latitudes of choice. Bloch underlined the crucial significance of catch-ing even a glimpse of visions of alterity: "But the fairy tale does not allow itself to be fooled by the present owners of Paradise. Thus, it is a rebel-lious, burned child and alert. One can climb a beanstalk up into heaven and then see how angels make gold" (1988b:169).

In landraces, folk varieties, and archaic cultigens that are maintained despite the fact that they are no longer (or never were) economically profitable, we find cultural conduits bridging the past and the present and providing just enough dissonance to sustain and congeal what Bloch referred to as the "not-yet-conscious" or the "yet-to-become." Consti-tuting a different but related form of colportage, these discordant notes serve as sensory reminders of meals cooked and meals shared, rituals participated in with kith and kin, and relief provided for major and mi-nor traumas and indignities of life. Jacques Barrau (cited in Dove 1999) referred to foxtail millet and Job's tears—archaic cultigens that continue to be grown, mainly for ritual purposes, in upland Southeast Asia—as "witnesses of the past." Like a stand of sugarcane on the Georgia coast

or a field of *oca* and *mashua* on the Andean slope, these witnesses of the
past crop up where they are not supposed to be, jolt us into attention,
and thereby call into serious question the inevitability of surrendering
all options to modernity. The same is true for traditional varieties of
crops such as rice, wheat, corn, potatoes, and sweet potatoes that continue to be planted in home gardens or at the fringes of commercial
plots, even in regions of the developing world dominated by the research
and extension model of international, and national, agricultural development. The persistence of these varieties underlines the possibility of
maintaining biological and cultural diversity and demonstrates the viability of on-the-ground, taken-for-granted forms of resistance embedded in countermemory. The life histories of seedsavers show how
countervailing sentiments embodied in their everyday lives allow people
to pick on the vulnerabilities of "monocultures of the mind."

Countermemory triggers reconnection to our past and our inner
selves by subverting dominant messages that tend to deny identity and
sense of place. These messages are more and more insistent and compelling.
They infiltrate our consciousness as they come from the outside and
from above in the form of global imperatives and trends. But a potent
counter emanates deep inside and refuses surrender. As Yael Zerubavel
wrote in *Recovered Roots:*

> The alternative commemorative narrative, operating under and
> against this hegemony, thus constitutes *countermemory*. . . . If the
> master commemorative narrative attempts to suppress alternative
> views of the past, the countermemory in turn denies the validity of
> the narrative constructed by collective memory and presents its own
> claim for a more accurate representation of history. This challenge
> not only addresses the symbolic realm, but obviously has direct po-
> litical implications. The master commemorative narrative represents
> the political elites' construction of the past which serves its special
> interests and promotes its political agenda. Countermemory chal-
> lenges this hegemony by offering a different commemorative narra-
> tive representing the views of marginalized individuals or groups
> within society. (1995:10–11)

On one level, the stage of power is secured through hegemonic narratives and the counter is likewise cast in unruly discourse and events. Local historians, shamans, storytellers, and, in their own way, present-day advocates and activists formulate these counternarratives and keep them circulating (Rappaport 1990; Comaroff and Comaroff 1993; Steedly 1993; Tsing 1993; Abercombie 1998; Cole 1998); they are what Connerton (1989:15) referred to as "relentless recorders" of unofficial, suppressed histories whose goal is to keep future generations from forgetting. In the case of seedsavers and heirloom gardeners, however, this subversion has less to do with narrative and discourse, even events, and more with visceral embodiment in *sites of memory*. These are not the ones found in rarefied memorials or museums, as sites and works of memory are normally understood, but those located in pulsating senses, germinating seeds, and thriving gardens, not to mention steaming kitchens and brimming tables. It is primarily in this warm, tantalizing sphere, rather than inscription in text, that they continue to keep creative options alive and salient. Paul Stoller referred to this sphere as the "sensory arena of countermemory," the "arena of fragrance and movement" (1995:35) and likened it to "an electric current that jolts bodies as they are charged and recharged by the social memories that define and redefine our beings in the world" (1995:198). The reverberations of countermemory through senses and emotions impact us above and beyond the capability of history or ideology, whether made or in the making.

Thus the apparently unstoppable loss of diversity that modernity and globalization entail is far from a foregone conclusion. In fact, if we follow Bloch's injunction to seek "estrangement from the familiar" so that we may "define things for ourselves," we will come to the realization that it is to some extent a blown-up straw man—the conceptual equivalent of the emperor's new clothes—and may it always remain so. Virtually by a fundamental physical law of action and reaction, force and counterforce, elements of marginality and resistance are part and parcel of any hegemony. Operating like transposable elements and colporteurs, these unorganized, intractable elements persist and act largely by awakening possibilities, deploying alternatives, and thereby maintaining a reservoir of diversity and flexibility. Writing on the dialectics of modernity,

John and Jean Comaroff noted that contrary to widespread and well-argued predictions that Western hegemony, through the synergistic mechanisms of markets, money, and media, will reduce the world to "numbing sameness," reality has in many instances proven otherwise. Quoting Louis McNiec, they observed that global systems of capital, ideology, and representation have to this day remained "incorrigibly plural." Insightfully, they remind us:

> Looked up close, then, modernity itself all too rapidly melts into air. As an analytical term, it becomes especially vague when dislodged from the ideal-typical, neo-evolutionary theoretical frame that classically encased it, defining it less in reference to the "real" world than by contrast to that other chimera, "tradition." Such binary contrasts, we would argue, are a widespread trope of ideology-in-the-making; they reduce the complex continuities and contradictions to the aesthetics of nice oppositions. (1993:xii)

Beyond Linearity

Very simply (perhaps too simply) put, Barbara McClintock's contribution to genetics is the recognition that genes can dissociate and actively transpose instead of being static, linear structures on the chromosome. I say perhaps too simply put because her contribution, or rather its belated recognition, was wrenched out of a highly charged milieu pitting individual creativity with scientific dogma. What may have helped was a certain degree of marginality in how she went about her work. According to a recent book on her life and her science, "McClintock could challenge the canonical view of the gene . . . because she was not bound by dogma as other geneticists were. She attended to her corn plants with sensitivity, even empathy. Free from the ossified theory that constrained other scientists' vision, she could see what others could not: genes are dynamic, interactive, flexible" (Comfort 2001:1–2).

For his part, Ernest Bloch's contribution to philosophy is the appreciation of concrete historical moments that shock us and give us pause and thereby open up avenues for reassessment and change. Bloch was perpetually rebellious against the dreariness, predictability, and orthodoxy of his own middle-class upbringing—all the bad aspects of which he lumped together as "mush"—as well as the dismissiveness of mainstream Marxism regarding colportage. Zipes explained that, "Bloch liked to generate a sense of *Stauner* in his readers. In German, *Stauner* implies not only startlement but astonishment, wonder, staring, and the formation of his philosophical categories compels us to pause and reconsider what we think, where we are, and what we want to look for" (1988:xxxi).

Aside from McClintock's and Bloch's strong personal traits of integrity and independence, their intellectual legacies—transposable elements and colportage—have indeed shocked, startled, and shaken their respective disciplines to their very core. I have chosen to employ these metaphors for seedsavers because I am convinced that we need a major pause to break away from discursive and strategic folds into which we have settled and to free ourselves from blocks of categories and hierarchies from which we draw our understanding of the world. In the field of plant genetic resources conservation, the danger is not in repeating ourselves so much as in imposing our schemas and designs on the margins and thereby thwarting what may be the last stronghold of biodiversity. A fundamental change in our conceptual metaphors will enable us to venture beyond Enlightenment—and the linear, totalizing thinking that dominates it—into more tenuous concerns dealing with indeterminacy, complexity, and emergence. This paradigm shift has been in the works for some time now and I will attempt a rough sketch of some pertinent intellectual developments before I close this chapter on conceptual metaphors.

Needless to say, systems that are more amenable to analysis, generalization, and prediction are more convenient. It is precisely for these qualities that the machine analogy and cybernetic model have stayed around for a long time. However, systems, even neat ones, are in a constant state of perturbation, or chaos. Changes build over time until a state of disequilibrium is reached. At this juncture, the cumulative challenge emanating from the changes can no longer be accommodated by the system. Irreversible processes build up, a point of bifurcation is reached, and a new "systemness" comes into being. Venturing away from homeostasis and equilibrium, chaos theory emphasized perturbations and change (Nicolis and Prigogine 1977, 1989; Prigogine and Stengers 1984). Building on chaos theory, a new science of complexity has emerged as the domain in between linearly determined order and indeterminate chaos (Waldorp 1992). Siegfried Streufert has an interesting way of putting it:

> The Newtonian system has served us well in all mechanistic endeavors. It allowed for the Industrial Revolution. It got us to the moon and back. Yet, again and again, we have failed to predict interrelated complex phenomena in the world around us. The economy continues to confound prediction. Psychology cannot explain human behavior. We do not know why, during a relatively short period of time in the history of the Earth, there was an explosion of life forms. When we do not have explanations, when our predictions fail, is it merely because we have not yet developed an adequate or complete understanding? Is it because our theories do not yet cover the basic clockwork of behavior? Hardly. (1997:2073)

A post-Newtonian revolution has been fomenting in recent years in fields as diverse as physics, biology, ecology, geography, psychology, and economics, bringing about a dramatic reformulation of ideas about equilibrium, causation, climax, and systemness itself under the rubric of complexity theory (see Nicolis and Prigogine 1977; Prigogine and Stengers 1984; Goodwin 1994; Byrne 1998; Manson 2001). This rethinking encompasses both the phenomena and the epistemology from which it is approached. Recognized more as a "scientific amalgam," a "rhetorical hybrid," rather than a singular epistemological position, complexity theory represents "a shift towards understanding the properties of interaction of systems as more than the sum of their parts . . . a science of qualities as much as of quantities" (Thrift 1999:33). In neuroscience, for instance, it has been proposed that complexity may account for how the dynamic "mind" arises from the structural "brain" through the evolution of neurons with "adaptive, multi-stable dynamical properties" (Koch and Laurent 1999:96), while in economics, complexity theory has been invoked to explain a range of intriguing phenomena from market instabilities, to emergence of monopolies, to persistence of vicious cycles of poverty (Arthur 1999). In ecology, an eclectic discipline to begin with, complexity theory is opening up opportunities to investigate the role of redundancy, entropy, and selection in nonlinear, dynamic, and self-organizing systems (Milne 1998). Correspondingly, researchers in other fields are reexamining basic premises of normative science, beginning with the most deeply entrenched ones of reducibility of all phenomena to its component parts and mechanistic operation in a lawful universe, and converging on a sentiment best, if lightly, expressed by Brian Arthur when he noted that "logic and philosophy are messy, that language is messy, that physics is messy, and finally that the economy is naturally messy. And it's not that this is a mess created by the dirt that's on the microscope glass. It's that this mess is inherent in the systems themselves" (cited in Waldorp 1993:329).

Increasing recognition of complexity is driven by a build-up of negative reaction to reductio ad absurdum, or obsessive reductionism, in science (Gallagher and Appenzeller 1999). Reductive thinking is dangerous in two ways. First, there is a tendency to boil down interesting and inherently complex phenomena into their component parts and force an explanation of the whole in terms of its parts. Second, and in my view more pernicious, is the tendency, particularly in the social sciences, to avoid or dismiss important and challenging questions that do not yield to this arbitrary and heavy-handed treatment, thus unwittingly limiting our exploration to what has been referred to in anthropology as "the science of trivia." In plant genetic resources research and conservation (including in situ initiatives), reductionism is expressed in efforts to straightjacket the rather exuberant fan of values and meanings attached by humans to the living world that surrounds them and from which they draw strength and sustenance. Such efforts, to my mind, are misguided as they grossly underestimate and oversimplify the underlying attachments and relationships. Instead of "commensuration" that demands standardization of disparate things, conversion of absolute differences to differences of degree, and reduction of the relevance of context (Espeland and Stevens 1998), Western knowledge and rationality must admit that other knowledges and cosmologies are of equal validity and worth. What would it take to transform a science that does violence to diversity and complexity to one that nurtures the fluorescence and resilience of life?

Although a "final theory" leading to a universal strategy might be highly desirable in the case of biodiversity conservation as in many others, such a pursuit is ultimately unrealistic and counterproductive. As Steven Weinberg, Nobel laureate in physics and author of *Dreams of a Final Theory* (1993), acknowledged, "While [a final theory] would be of unlimited validity and entirely satisfying in its completeness and consistency, . . . wonderful phenomena, from turbulence to thought, would still need explanation, whatever final theory is discovered" (1993:3). Somewhere between turbulence and thought are the enigmatic proclivities of mind and behavior that undergird seedsaving and conservation through use of landraces or folk varieties. From the perspective of complexity—and drawing on the metaphors of jumping genes and colporteurs presented in this chapter—perhaps we can come to a better understanding of nonlinear relationships between dynamic entities, the qualitative and oftentimes symbolic nature of interactions, and the emergence of novel, synergistic properties from localized nodes and embedded networks that make this possible.

Farmers and gardeners from different parts of the world have made persistent and significant contributions to the conservation of biodiversity. Inconspicuous and nonthreatening like jumping genes, they blend into the margins and work the borders, continuing in their uncaptured ways despite the powerful pull of modernity. Curious and playful like itinerant colporteurs, they challenge the normative landscape and the predictable flow of history with their lifestyles and their collections. Through irreverence, possibly more than resistance, they make prevailing orthodoxies like economies of scale that demand ever-increasing commercialization and homogenization less of a given and more of a starting point for reflection and transformation. Through embodiment rather than inscription—in other words, by parlaying powerful sensory stimuli rather than elaborate and at times obtuse rhetoric—they foreground diverse, viable alternatives that otherwise could be forgotten and lost. By continuing to use their land, time, and energy in cultivating and exchanging a wide array of plants, and obviously enjoying it, they poke fun at the twin demigods of modernity—productivity and efficiency—and whittle away at their facade of invincibility. In a very real sense, they challenge the normative assumptions of linearity and progress by their very presence. In so doing, they counter despair and offer hope. I believe that the choices and possibilities they force us to confront can help us overcome what at times can only be interpreted as an unfortunate failure of nerve.

Ordinary/
Extraordinary Lives

. . . .

In order to re-present the "space on the side of the road" then, we need more than assertions that the local has its own epistemology or that everything is culturally constructed. We need to approach the clash of epistemologies—ours and theirs—and to use that clash to repeatedly re-open a gap in the theory of culture so that we can imagine culture as constituted in use.

—Kathleen Stewart, *A Space on the Side of the Road*

For however partial or even mistaken the experienced reality of the human agents, it is that experienced reality that provides the basis for their understanding and their action.

—James C. Scott, *Weapons of the Weak*

Seedsavers comprise an obscure but omnipresent challenge to agricultural commercialization, monoculture, and genetic erosion. Because of their marginality and random distribution, they elude the more quantitative studies on conservation of crop genetic resources in which assumptions of intrapopulation homogeneity and rule-based behavior still prevail for the most part. Some notable exceptions to this bias in the literature are cited in the discussion that follows, but my intention in presenting our research findings is to highlight the role of qualitative experience and memory in the unlikely persistence of traditional, nonprofitable, and "obsolete" folk varieties in small-scale fields and gardens. Seedsavers embroider landscapes of forgetting and abandonment with sensory reminders of identity and alterity. Thus, they provoke the rest of us to examine with fresh vision the vulnerabilities of modernity and globalization and to take stock of our own options. Their diverse farms, gardens, and seed collections are like unexpected cleavages in a spreading surrender of will to an overwhelming and diffuse power.

How is this resistance possible? Indeed, as James Ferguson pointed out, "The place from which power is exercised is often a hidden place. When we try to pin it down, the center always appears to be somewhere else. Yet we know that this phantom center, elusive as it is, exerts a real, undeniable power over the whole social framework of our culture, and over the ways we think about it" (1990:9). From my perspective, the phantom center may have undeniable power but it is far from omnipotent. For one thing, it is "outnumbered"; the margins always border the center, more expansive in both absolute and relative terms. Oftentimes, the center is also "outwitted" by the margins—its elements more supple, more nimble, more hidden, and more complex. Nineteenth-century France, for instance, was characterized by repressive state control of the popular press. Censorship laws suppressed a good deal of political opposition, driving publishers to bankruptcy, prison, or underground. Bourgeois standards determined what was socially or politically dangerous, and transgressions were seized, banned, or fined accordingly. And yet, at the level of France's cheaper and more marginal popular press, clever printers and colporteurs took advantage of the system's weaknesses, evading fines, resisting arrest and closure, and on the whole making sure that dissent was alive and well through a clandestine web of publishing and circulating reading materials directed at the masses. It did not help that the police and the censors, because of corruption and indifference, failed to enforce the most important censorship laws of the land (Cragin 2001).

The tension between the center and the margins is evident in the centripetal suction toward uniformity and the centrifugal pull toward diversity with regards to many of the world's important crops. Impressed with the quality and size of certain crops he encountered in his travels, the pioneering plant collector Nikolai Vavilov recognized the centripetal attraction for crop improvement, but he did not equally emphasize the tensions and trade-offs between the divergent forces when he wrote:

> The world's *chef d'ouvre* of plant breeding is to be found on the is-
> land of Sukarajima in southern Japan: a radish one *pud* in weight
> [fifteen to seventeen kilograms]. On the same island under condi-
> tions similar to those in which it thrives, are wild radish and a culti-
> vated radish, each related to the same botanical species, which form
> only small roots. It would be vain then to ask how the wonderful
> giant has been produced; no one knows, not even the professor of
> plant breeding who lives on the neighboring island of Kagoshima.
> But one thing is certain, the giant forms were the consequence of
> skillful selection of extreme variants by unknown breeders many
> ages ago. An interesting principle is deducible from a comparison of
> ancient farming civilizations; the higher the technical level of a popu-
> lation the more highly bred are its crops. Thus, Chinese vegetables
> including different varieties of cabbage, soybeans, rice, and many
> crops of Mediterranean countries, where the powerful civilizations
> of the Old World once thrived, are noteworthy for quality and size
> of fruit and seed, and altogether bear witness of careful selection
> during many centuries. . . . On the other hand, in many regions in
> northwest India, Afghanistan, and Abyssinia, and in Peru and Bo-
> livia among the pre-Inca civilizations preserved in the mountainous
> regions of the Andes, the plant varieties are small, unfruitful, poor
> in quality, and but little different from the wild forms which often
> grew in fields nearby, in uncultivated land and field borders. (Vavilov
> 1951:2)

Note that even the most gigantic and impressive of Vavilov's examples were bred through careful selection carried out by local experts and there-fore qualify as landraces in contrast to advanced or purebred lines. Along-side these important landraces, however, are "the wild forms which of-ten grew in fields nearby" (small and unfruitful though they may be) that need to be conserved in situ in those marginal spaces or ex situ in scientifically managed gene banks.

Blight in the Wilderness

In modern commercial agriculture, national and international research and development agenda as well as markets are so powerful that they practically dictate what varieties farmers will plant. Credit and insurance are predicated on the use of one to a few recommended varieties in many developing countries. The profit motive can be so flagrant that, in many instances, offices where agricultural loans are processed and disbursed are the same places where recommended seeds, fertilizers, and pesticides are sold. This system of sanctions and incentives has been extremely effective in predisposing the present production system to uniformity and instability. What little choice is left after insurance and credit requirements are met is further constrained by the synchrony and consensus imposed by the biological and economic rhythms dictated by modern high-yielding varieties. But developed country agriculture is not exempt from this homogenization. A notorious example, the Southern corn blight of the early 1970s, devastated American farmers "from Maine to Miami, from Mobile to Moline" (National Academy of Sciences 1972), causing them to lose their harvest, and in some cases their farms. This sweeping epidemic was a blight on the record of the premier land grant-based agricultural research and development system in the world and called attention to some of its vulnerabilities.

At the root of the Southern corn blight tragedy was the farmers' dependence on genetically identical, or relatively uniform, varieties. Whereas diverse mixtures carry an array of resistant genes and are well-buffered such that pest infestations rarely reach epidemic proportions, Southern corn fields were extremely vulnerable to any pathogen or prey that happened to strike. After much finger pointing, an aggressive breeding program was launched to find a solution to a catastrophe that was brought on by earlier experiments to improve the high-yielding corn, ironically by using a sterile male cytoplasm derived from a modern Texas cultivar that promised to endow greater over-all resistance—according to Michael Hoffman, H. David Thurston, and Margaret E. Smith (1993), it was supposed to be virtually "pathogen-proof." It is notable that what saved the day was the little-known *Mayorbala* maize from Africa (Fowler and Mooney 1990). Though initially unimpressive, traditional varieties and wild relatives of crops that are mainly nurtured at the periphery of commercial agriculture or in gene banks comprise a repository of last resort.

In Asia, traditional aromatic strains of rice were disease resistant and tall enough to shade out weeds. Hence, they did not require much by way of inputs or maintenance. However, their stalks bent or lodged in strong wind and when treated with a surfeit of fertilizer—a not-too-minor problem for intensive or high-input agriculture. So the modern rice cultivars were bred to be uniformly dwarf or semidwarf, with abbreviated stalks that can hold fertilizers and translate these to heavy panicles that signaled greater yield and profit. However, much of the rice-growing zones in Asia are in the flood plains, where short-statured, input-dependent cultivars face serious drawbacks. Meanwhile, distributed in the marshy areas of tropical and subtropical Asia is a wild rice species, *Oryza rufipogon*, which is the progenitor of Asian cultivated rice, *Oryza sativa*. According to Masahiro Akimoto and his coworkers (1999), this wild progenitor has wide resistance to diseases and pests, and strong deep-water tolerance, and produces fertile hybrids with F1 cultivars. For these reasons, it is considered an important genetic resource for rice breeding. Unfortunately, destruction of their marginal habitats by human activity and genetic contamination from modern cultivars, also introduced by human activity, threaten the genes of *Oryza rufipogon* and other wild relatives.

The Southern corn blight and the Asian rice progenitor, though coming at the problem from different directions, illustrate a few important lessons that I believe have wider applicability. First is the dependence of the center, in this case formal agricultural research and development, on the margins for plant genetic resources that buoy its breeding programs, providing a reliable form of crop insurance, particularly when the unforeseen strikes. Without landraces and wild relatives to draw upon, there would be no way to improve varieties or play catch-up with unexpected outcomes of these improvements. Second is the existence of heavy trade-offs as scientists aim for greater productivity. The introduction of a desired trait could spawn a host of undesirable consequences (in other words, no free lunch). Third is the reality that the margins are permeable and vulnerable to "centering" (in other words, we *can* kill the goose that lays the golden eggs). In the case of corn, landraces in centers of diversity are being contaminated through introgression from transgenic introductions (Kloppenburg 1988; Kamm-Gordon et al. 1999). In the case of *Oryza rufipogon*, habitat disturbance from livestock grazing and road construction as well as contamination from industrial discharge and modern agriculture reduced a population that was viable in 1985 to complete extinction by 1996 (Akimoto, Shimamoto, and Morishima 1999). With spreading blight, a categorical gloom is all too easy to perceive. However, I prefer to dwell on the pinpoints of light, which are present and relevant as well.

Seedsavers of the Global South

I begin by discussing some aspects of the life histories of farmers and gardeners that I, along with Robert Rhoades and our students, research assistants, and "memory bankers," have documented in the context of five research projects over a period of approximately fifteen years (see table). In addition to a concentration on local knowledge and plant genetic resources management and conservation, what connects these research projects as well as our informants and collaborators is a shared location in the global South—the less developed counterpart of the more highly industrialized core, whether at the global, regional, or national scale. In relation to biodiversity, the South is also regarded as "gene-rich" but "technology-poor" vis-à-vis the North's status as "gene-poor" but "technology-rich." This kind of assessment, while partially accurate, rationalizes a global division of labor that marginalizes diverse landraces of the South as nothing more than raw materials for plant breeding and biotechnology in the North. In short, the places and people I will discuss are all relatively peripheral or marginal in a multilayered and intricately nested world system. As varied and idiosyncratic as their responses are to this marginalization, they share some interesting attributes, supporting bell hooks's contention that "marginality is much

TABLE. Summary of Research Projects and Their Parameters

Research	Location	Time Period	Organization
Cultivators in Transition: Operational Reality and Cognized Models in Agricultural Decision Making	Kabaritan, the Philippines	1986–87	Ford Foundation, International Rice Research Institute
Memory Banking of Indigenous Knowledge Associated with Traditional Crop Varieties	Bukidnon, the Philippines	1990–92	User's Perspective with Agricultural Research and Development, International Potato Center
Southern Seed Legacy	Southern United States	1995–present	Sustainable Agriculture Research and Education Consortium
Comparative Ethnoecology and Biodiversity Enhancement in Watersheds and Buffer Zones Ethnoecology of Fragile Lands in the Andes	Nanegal and Cotacachi, Ecuador	1997–present	Sustainable Agriculture and Natural Resource Management Collaborative Research Support Program
Introduced Germplasm from Vietnam: Documentation, Acquisition, and Preservation	Georgia and Florida	2001–present	Agricultural Research Service, U.S. Department of Agriculture

more than a site of deprivation . . . it is also a site of resistance" (1990:342). I will proceed by describing these various research projects and then introduce the seedsavers who captivated and intrigued me in each of them.

In the research project Cultivators in Transition, I focused on agricultural decision making of different categories of rural cultivators in Kabaritan, a village in the town of Bay, located in the province of Laguna, the Philippines (Nazarea-Sandoval 1995). Kabaritan (fig. 8) is a lakeshore farming community bordering Laguna de Bay, the largest freshwater lake in the Philippines. From the early 1970s to the mid-1980s, Kabaritan underwent a rapid socioeconomic and demographic transition driven by three major developments: the adoption of Green Revolution varieties and technologies, the implementation of land reform, and the introduction of a new livelihood strategy, *Tilapia nilotica* aquaculture. Unlike traditional rice cultivation, the Green Revolution demanded more input, and hence more capital, thus favoring bigger landowners despite its claim of scale neutrality. Further, while rice cultivation sharply delineated landowners from landless tenants or casual laborers, raising tilapia "fingerlings" or fries in fishponds did not require a significant or secure land base. Landless tenants and migrants as well as fishermen could squat on idle land or act as caretakers for absentee fishpond owners or agents of fingerlings. Consequently, from a sharp distinction based on landownership and occupation, socioeconomic classes blurred to a combination of landed rice farmers, land reform beneficiaries, tenants, landless migrants, and part-time fishpond operators and agents. It was in Kabaritan where I met Braulio de Villa, a local healer who lived on top of an abandoned railroad track bordering an irrigated rice-aquaculture farming system. Landless and living, quite literally, on the fringe of Kabaritan, Mang Braulio was village sage and village clown, all at the same time ("Mang" and "Aling" are titles of respect for older men and women in the Philippines).

In Intavas and Salvacion in Bukidnon, the Philippines (fig. 9), I sought to develop and put to use a method for documenting traditional varieties of sweet potatoes and associated local knowledge, which I called memory banking. By systematically investigating the local beliefs and practices

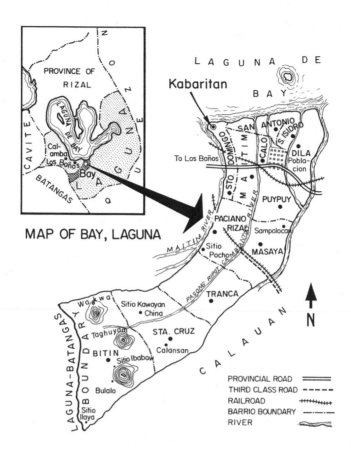

Figure 8 Study areas in Kabaritan, the Philippines (Source: Nazarea-Sandoval 1995)

that undergird biological diversity of culturally significant plants, memory banking can run parallel to gene banking in conserving plant genetic resources (Nazarea 1998). Intavas is a remote upland area populated mainly by the indigenous Bukidnons who cultivate sweet potatoes on a subsistence scale. According to the natives, Intavas was once populated by warring tribes whose territories were marked off by thick stands of cogon, bamboo, rattan, and trees. Any transgressor was liable to get his head chopped off (*tavas*) if he tried to cross the boundary of wild vegetation

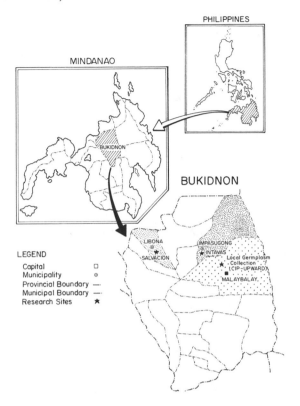

Figure 9 Study areas in Bukidnon, the Philippines (Source: Nazarea 1998)

between tribes. Others say the name comes from chopping down or clearing the formidable thicket that separated the tribes when they made peace. Salvacion, on the other hand, is more of what one would call a frontier town, relatively close to the market and to the pineapple plantation of the multinational Del Monte Corporation. *Dumagats* (literally, from across the seas) or migrants from other islands of the Philippines who were seeking land, or fleeing from the Japanese soldiers during World War II, referred to the area as their "salvation" when they came upon it.

At the time of my research in the early 1990s, sweet potato production was becoming commercialized in Salvacion but was still predominantly at the subsistence level in Intavas. However, the difference was one of degree and not of kind. One of the objectives of the memory banking project was to study the effect of commercialization on cultural and genetic diversity, my main hypothesis being that commercialization causes a significant narrowing of genetic and cultural diversity in relation to sweet potato production. As expected, I found that genetic diversity, as measured by the number of sweet potato varieties planted, was narrower in Salvacion than in Intavas (albeit with only a slight difference of three varieties). But, surprisingly, I discovered a marked disparity between the two sites in terms of the number of varieties known or remembered (a difference of eighteen), indicating a faster attrition of cultural knowledge or, more specifically, cognition of diversity, than erosion of genetic diversity itself. It signified to me that in the context of agricultural development and market integration, knowledge may actually be the first to go (Nazarea 1998).

In Intavas, Maricel Piniero, my research assistant, and I met Francisca Bactol, a subsistence-oriented farmer native to the area who continued to plant the sweet potato varieties, along with other edible plants that her parents had grown with nearly the same cultural practices before her. In Salvacion we met Matias Benting, a more commercialized producer who migrated to Bukidnon from another island when he was a young man. Despite the obvious differences between an indigenous female subsistence farmer, who hardly moved in her lifetime, and an itinerant male commercial producer, who had lived in many of the surrounding islands and tried his hand at various occupations, the difference in inclination toward saving traditional varieties of sweet potatoes was not as significant as I had suspected, or hoped for given my hypothesis. Nor were their motivations totally disparate for, although to a different degree and with different representativeness, even the commercial farmer retained varieties that were not favored by the market and exerted effort to source them out and keep them in his farm.

In the context of the Southern Seed Legacy, aimed at conserving both seeds and memories of Southern heirloom gardeners and farmers in the United States, my coworkers and I met many individuals who saved, exchanged, and talked about seeds, mainly for pleasure and remembrance (figs. 10 and 11). While several seed companies and nurseries—even those that, inspired by the environmental movement,

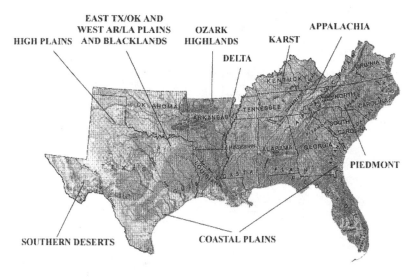

SELECTED AGROECOREGIONS IN THE SOUTH

Figure 10 Agroecoregions of the American South (Source: Robert Rhoades and Virginia Nazarea, Southern Seed Legacy Proposal, 1996)

were specializing in native and traditional varieties—were successfully preserving and marketing seeds of old varieties of edible and ornamental plants, little attention, credit, and support were being given to the seedsavers and gardeners who had conserved these seeds and kept them in circulation for generations. We also noted that formal and/or commercial seedsaving organizations did not have a very strong presence in our region and slowly it dawned on us why. The American South is a special place where many of the "old-fashioned" values are still very much intact, in fact unabashedly flaunted. The home and the garden are central to the Southern sense of place—a hearty "Ya'll come back and see us, ya' hear" is frequently heard instead of "Good-bye, stay in touch"— and, in this milieu, seeds connect people to place and past to present. Clearly, an impersonal seedsaving system would be superfluous and out of place.

Through the Southern Seed Legacy Project, and in particular through our committed students and energetic "memory bankers," I met some

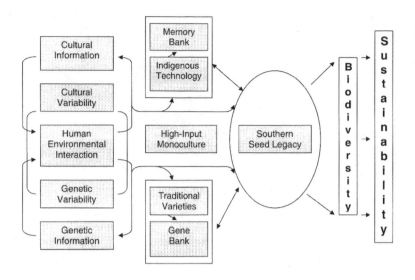

Figure 11 Conceptual framework of the Southern Seed Legacy Project

interesting individuals who have saved seeds and planted gardens year after year. In Kentucky, Mattie Arnett and her brother, Luther Risner, are still connected to a kin-based, memory-laden traffic of corn, peas, and beans originating from their homeplace in Morgan County in eastern Kentucky even after the family had dispersed and they themselves had moved to Verona, in northern Kentucky near Cincinnati. Fanny Lou Bryan of Dahlonega, Georgia, had not only been saving but was also selling seeds of "fragrant plumgranny" and a special kind of white cucumber far and wide for nearly two decades since she became a widow. Then there was Ernest Keheley, a farmer/mechanic in his eighties who lived in the same farmhouse where he was born and raised. His place is surrounded and nearly engulfed by the urban sprawl of Marietta, Georgia, his garden an anachronism among his new neighbors' neatly manicured lawns. In the Gullah-Geechee community of Hog Hammock on Sapelo Island, Georgia, Vi Johnson and Allen Green cultivate and exchange seeds of favorite varieties of peas, beans, and greens that have sustained them, their children, and their children's children through the seasons of their lives. In Clinton, Tennessee, Rudolph and Helen

Humphrey are still saving some pumpkin and bean varieties that have been with them since they started gardening while at the same time lamenting the loss of "old-timey" sugarcane varieties. The life histories of these Southern seedsavers reveal a passion for things out of the ordinary, a yearning for connection to their past.

Yet another project arose from my exposure to a concentration on heirloom gardeners who are not indigenous to the American South. Vietnamese immigrant-gardeners like Nhan Nguyen Couch and Thanh Nguyen (not related) in rural areas and urban centers of the Southern United States became part of a new research initiative on the documentation, acquisition, and preservation of introduced germplasm from Vietnam. Nhan came to the United States to protect her son from the reprisal she believed would be forthcoming because he is half-American; Thanh came as a political refugee because of his military involvement during the war. Despite the availability of many Vietnamese vegetables, fruit, and herbs in Asian markets, immigrants still cultivate these crops in their backyard gardens for reasons related to memory, identity, and place. The purpose of the Vietnamese germplasm research is to document and help conserve the plants that were introduced to the United States through Vietnamese immigration, notably from 1975 onward, but what really fascinated me were the immigrants' motivations behind the conservation of these seeds.

Migrants and seeds often go together, each transporting seemingly indispensable to the other. This was certainly true of Jose Valverde, whom we met in Nanegal, Ecuador, while doing interdisciplinary research in the Andean site of a global project under the Sustainable Agriculture and Natural Resources Management Collaborative Research Support Program (fig. 12). Our part, the Ethnoecology component, pursued both basic and applied questions pertaining to land use change and biodiversity management in watersheds, forest reserves, and buffer zones. Don Jose was a migrant from Colombia—a farmer who tried to find a peaceful place to live and work near a nature reserve. Surprisingly, he turned out to be an incorrigible collector of all kinds of seeds, his house a veritable seed bank.

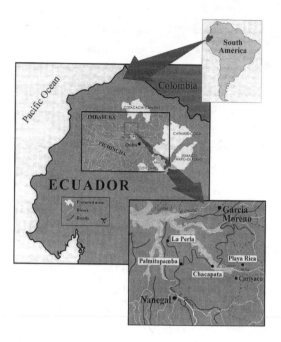

Figure 12   Nanegal, Ecuador (Source: Robert Rhoades, *Bridging Human and Ecological Landscapes: Participatory Research and Sustainable Development in an Andean Agricultural Frontier* [Dubuque, Iowa: Kendall/Hunt Publishing Company, 2001])

Vernacular Visionaries

There is at least one person in every village who everyone recognizes as being out of the ordinary—the local sage, or perhaps the village clown; the lines are blurred. As every anthropologist knows, when entering a new field site there is frequently someone who gingerly or boldly steps out of the crowd, unable to contain his or her curiosity and eager to explore the world of the stranger and impart some vision of his or her own. Independent and idiosyncratic, seedsavers generally belong in this category. Their life histories are richly varied in contextual particularities and, one might add, personality quirks. Yet their characteristics and actions cut across cultural and geographical boundaries. The stories included here portray how they have negotiated the terrains of their existence, particularly with reference to the diversity of crops that they have nurtured and used through time. These individuals are ordinary and extraordinary at the same time; ordinary in the sense that they can be found in practically any type of small-scale agricultural system yet also extraordinary in the sense that they stand out among their peers because of certain inclinations that I will try to bring into focus.

What, one may ask, is the value of ordinary lives? When the issue is of global import and urgency, such as genetic erosion of staple crops, or the extinction of life on the planet as we know it, is there any significance of seedsaver stories beyond the anecdotal? In presenting an account of the lives of seedsavers, I include details not normally included in a parsimonious scientific work because of my desire to convey the texture and serendipity of these encounters. In weaving these stories together, I see the warp as actions of an everyday or quotidian nature, those that penetrate and reverberate without much effort or much contest, and the crosswise woof as the extraordinary impact of these innocuous actions as reflective utopias that constitute a powerful countermemory. Together, the warp and woof make for the unintended role of seedsavers as *visionaries in the vernacular*. In this role, they either stand out or fade into the larger, more visible, and occasionally acrimonious backdrop.

Biodiversity conservation has been approached as a scientific problem first and a policy mandate second (although it can be argued with some justification that it is, in fact, the other way around). Since the first call to arms in the 1980s, biological and social scientists have been analyzing causes and trends and fashioning solutions. More recently, biodiversity has been recast in the constructivist sense as a specter of an environmental workhorse under threat and, in conservation, as a nascent social movement with broader political ends—a renegotiation of the dominant discourse on nature and culture that reinforces the interconnectivity among identity and ethnicity, territoriality, autonomy, and natural resource claims (Takacs 1996; Escobar 1998; Hayden 2003). These claims and counterclaims travel across various locations and conversations and in no time assume a life of their own (certainly a language of their own), not unlike the constructs they critique. On the other hand, while the concept of biodiversity is being deconstructed and its attendant issues debated on the big stage of science, technology, and society, while biologists and anthropologists ponder deeply and NGOs organize zealously, seedsavers go about their daily round—exchanging, renewing, and connecting through seeds and memories.

I am interested primarily in the vernacular nature of their contribution, in tracing how this ordinariness translates into something more deep-seated and trenchant than any intellectual discourse, organized movement, or policy initiative. While anthropologists have, in the last couple of decades, shaken off the confines of the village and the tribe and gone from the habitual micro to the more glamorous macro, I believe we should retain some ethnographic engagement in these crevices of creative human responses to modernity and globalization. This would, in my view, involve returning to things we care about and are good at and balancing multi-sited with deeply sited ethnography. Thus, seemingly mundane details are included here for a purpose: to convey the many facets of resistance to the homogenization inherent in monoculture that constitute conservation as a way of life and at the same time to support my argument that we seriously risk missing a lode of meaning and significance if we concentrate on streamlining our approaches, methods, and reports at the expense of lived experience and personal accounts. For this reason, I will recount these meandering stories and memories, beginning with the story of Mang Braulio.

A Matter of Taste, A Matter of Style

Landless and sanguine, Mang Braulio did not easily fit into any preconceived notions of "rural cultivators" (fig. 13). For one thing, unlike in the case of "normal" informants, I did not find him, he found me. I had been in Kabaritan for a couple of months when a tall, lean man in his sixties met me, grandchild in tow, halfway across one of the paddy bunds near the abandoned railroad track. He introduced himself as a caretaker for some tilapia fishponds for absentee owners, and I introduced myself as an anthropology graduate student doing research in his area. No further introductions were needed at that time, although I was to discover later on that he was also a local curer/herbalist who possessed knowledge

Figure 13 Braulio de Villa's motley collection of domesticated and wild plants bordering a rice field in Kabaritan, the Philippines (photo by author)

about nearly all the "good weeds," or wild herbs with curative potencies. He was also a keen observer of natural processes, with boundless curiosity. Despite not owning any farmland and having received little formal schooling, he knew the life habits of many different kinds of insects and spiders including when, in the life cycle of rice, they are most active or harmful. These attributes were doubtless sharpened by a life of struggle. He told me that as a young man, his wanderings were "directionless, like a mad dog." However, by his own account, he went wherever there were coconuts to harvest, or rice fields to plant and weed. Actually, he had been to Kabaritan several times when the railroad was still in use and before the existence of irrigation. That time they were still planting several different rice varieties in Kabaritan—aromatic, soft-textured, "slippery," and tasty varieties that he remembers quite well.

In the early 1970s, Mang Braulio and his extended family migrated to Kabaritan in search of some peace after having lived most of their lives in Quezon Province, known for its unequal (nearly feudal) land distribution, agrarian unrest, and accompanying military presence. His wife and children worked as casual laborers (summoned on a day-to-day basis by a *cabecilla*, or a female head of party), transplanting and weeding rice or scaring away birds from ripening grains at the nearby International Rice Research Institute (IRRI). Mang Braulio, because of his health, stayed closer to home, minding the tilapia fishponds and taking care of his grandchildren. In the town where he came from, according to Mang Braulio, "you never know if you'll make it to sunrise." Perhaps he found the situation in Kabaritan a little more stable, but he still likened landless farm laborers to "chaffs of rice that get blown every which way, depending on direction of the wind."

Why then did it seem to me that Mang Braulio was, within limits, quite capable of charting his own course? Under the caretaking arrangement, the fishpond owner provided all the inputs and the caretakers (in this case Mang Julio and his family) provided all the labor, receiving 20 percent of the entire sales from tilapia fingerlings at harvest time. This share he supplemented by diverting feed for the tilapia—actually nutritional supplements of milk and grits from the United States procured by the fishpond owner from the black market—to feed his grandchildren. This supplemented their daily diet of "rice with soy sauce, rice with sugar, rice with salt, or rice with fish sauce." He decided to acquire as much knowledge of herbal medicine as possible when three of his young children died of respiratory ailments in quick succession. He combined principles gleaned from health care training sponsored by the government at the village level with sacred practices learned from his "bible," the *Arte de Santa Maria* and the teachings of the Mystica cult. Because of this background, according to Mang Braulio, "I can interpret the sounds from the stethoscope, but I prefer to take the pulse to determine what ails the person."

Mang Braulio could name and describe the uses for the majority of the plants growing within a one-mile radius of his house and had lined his staircase with tin cans that contained mixtures of edible and medicinal plants collected and transplanted from the wild. He was articulate and knowledgeable not only about the curative value of these plants but also about their nutritive value and undesirable side effects. He concentrated

Figure 14 Francisca Bactol, from Bukidnon, the Philippines (photo by Maricel Piniero)

on the "wild side" because, as he explained to me, "if one plants vegetables in the backyard, they will be eaten by goats; if one raises chickens, they will be stolen by thieves, and it is the thieves who will get fat."
About two years after I left Kabaritan, I heard that Mang Braulio had
died, struck by lightning as he negotiated the bunds between rice fields.
Looking back, Mang Braulio's lifestyle was noticeable for its independence and tenacity, perhaps not only to me as an outsider but also to the
other "squatters" in the area—as landless, migrant laborers were referred to—and to the landed farmers and long-time tenants who oftentimes sought him out for his advice.

Unlike Mang Braulio, Francisca Bactol was born on the same parcel
of land that she still cultivated in Intavas, Bukidnon (fig. 14). She had
moved only once in her sixty-eight years, after the death of her first husband, who had been chosen for her by her parents, as was the custom in
those days. After she met her second husband, she moved back with
him to Intavas to resume farming. The native Bukidnons still comprised
the majority in Intavas despite considerable in-migration and intermarriage.

Figure 15 Francisca Bactol using blunt digging stick (photo by Maricel Piniero)

Agriculture was mostly small in scale except for the more intensive veg-etable farming that was introduced by migrants from the highlands of northern Luzon. Aling Francisca's parents, both native Bukidnons, were farmers who lived in the foothills of Mount Kitanglad and practiced slash-and-burn agriculture. They planted corn, bananas, taro, vegetables, and root crops, including sweet potatoes, as she was growing up. She and her husband have stuck with the same cropping combination, although they no longer practice shifting cultivation. She further explained that she always does the planting and harvesting of sweet potatoes herself "because I know sweet potatoes by heart."

Over the years, Aling Francisca has maintained agricultural prac-tices that followed closely on the methods and beliefs of her parents. She planted by the lunar cycle, seeing the full moon (*bitay*) as a good sign that the sweet potatoes will have "many and big roots." Moreover, she always planted four vines per "hill" or mound, "two to one side and two at the other," because she believed that the vines need to be spaced out in order to yield well. According to her, harvesting has to be done using

Figure 16 Matias Benting, from Salvacion, the Philippines (photo by Maricel Piniero)

a blunt stick, not a *bolo* (sharp, elongated knife), in order to prevent cutting the vines and damaging the roots (fig. 15). She carefully selected the bigger roots, staggering her harvest to two roots per hill, and returned the smaller roots to the ground, "so that we will have something to harvest in the next month." Although she planted a few hills of a variety called *lambayong* for the market, she also cultivated her favored varieties because she preferred "those varieties that are dry and very sweet like *si-uron*, while lambayong causes colic and is not my favorite. But, as of today, I still cultivate this variety along with *camba, kalibre,* and si-uron. This is to grow the 'best variety' and at the same time to be able to choose the variety that we want to cook based on our taste preference." Aside from sweet potatoes, Aling Francisca also grew corn, peanuts, taro, and cassava because "these crops support life, unlike cabbage, tomato, and bell pepper, whose prices go up and down . . . [hence] you cannot always get your capital back." She reported that rats and insect pests did "not do anything . . . we leave them alone because they cannot consume all the sweet potatoes anyway." In persisting in what her parents had taught her—time-tested knowledge and practices that often ran counter to the advice of outside experts—Aling Francisca maintained a certain degree of autonomy from market forces and extension agents that had penetrated Intavas despite its remoteness. Perhaps without meaning to, she also preserved options that might otherwise have fallen by the wayside in the course of modernization.

Matias Benting, who lived and farmed in Salvacion, was consistently philosophical, almost fatalistic, about the trials and the "hard blows" he had faced in life (fig. 16). Since his father died when he was very young, he attended school only until the second grade. His family was very poor, so he worked for some rich people in town, planting and tending corn, cassava, ginger, banana, vegetables, and sweet potatoes. He also revealed, "My wife always nagged me; hence, I always went away to other places. I did not want to get married at that age. I still would have liked to remain a bachelor but . . ." Mang Matias tried to "escape" by working in other provinces and trying his hand at various occupations, including fishing. In the course of his travels, he acquired a level of sophistication that was somewhat uncharacteristic of residents of his small village. One reflection of this sophistication was his extensive knowledge of sweet potato varieties and his sensitivity to the existence of nomenclatural confusion and redundancy pertaining to the different local varieties. Moreover, Mang Matias expressed awareness of genetic erosion or loss of varieties, even before the topic was broached:

> The varieties that we planted were *binangkal; kalugti*, which has elongated roots, white flesh, and white skin; *malunsai; kaborong*, which has yellow skin and white flesh and has a bland taste; *kuhit-guti*, which is also called *katapok*. We also had *kabato* and *tangkalon*, which has elongated roots and yellow flesh like egg yolk, but when it matures, the color is white. The *karunsing* variety never disappeared. The varieties that we are planting right now are *kabata*, which is also called *senorita; kamada; lila*, which has many colors in the flesh and leaves; five-finger and *initlog*. . . . There were other varieties like *martizans*, which have white flesh and skin like turnips and rounded roots as well; *magtapok*, which has small and many roots, red skin

and white flesh; *tangkalon*, which has elongated roots, white skin, and white flesh; and *magtuko*, which has red skin, white flesh, and elongated roots. But these sweet potatoes have disappeared already. We cannot find them anymore.

Mang Matias distinguished his personal taste from consumer preference or market demand, stating that he liked varieties that were sweet and dense, but consumers paid more attention to whether or not sweet potatoes were powdery. He further noted that no one had much tolerance for the watery varieties introduced by extension agents, so these were mostly fed to pigs. Having diversified his planting to include eggplant, bell pepper, and tomatoes—both for consumption and for sale—and prospered, he has come to the conclusion that "as long as a person is hard working in this place, he will not suffer or go hungry." Through his knowledge, and also by the fact that he continues to plant different crop varieties despite the integration of his farm to the market, he has helped keep diversity alive and perceptually salient in this commercializing area. Given that Mang Matias, at fifty-eight, was widely recognized as one of the most successful sweet potato farmers in Salvacion, his penchant for collecting and planting as many varieties as he can get his hands on must provoke some questions and sow some doubts about the presumed superiority of uniformity in the minds of other farmers in Salvacion (fig. 17).

Microchallenges to Modernity

In many parts of the Philippines, as in other developing countries, the Green Revolution legacy is most keenly felt in the simplification and control of lowland, irrigated rice-farming systems. This is manifested in the adoption and widespread use of one to a few modern cultivars; the importation and adherence to prescribed inputs of fertilizers, pesticides, and herbicides; and the acquired discipline of a regimen of transplanting, irrigating, and weeding. While I do not agree with the contention that "the simplifying tendencies of reductionist science have meshed well

Figure 17 Matias Benting's assorted sweet potato vines ready for planting (photo by
Maricel Piniero)

with the ecological and social simplicity of standardized, specialized farming systems" (Pimbert 1994:20), simplification continues to be the
leitmotif of development and, oddly enough at times, of conservation.
An integral part of this simplification is the need for a tight conceptual
design in plant breeding and genetic engineering to minimize the amount
of trial and error necessary to identify and combine (or, lately, insert)
desired traits to improve upon existing varieties.

As noted, the "success" of the Green Revolution, which tripled rice
yields in Asia (IRRI 1993), was based on the breeding of dwarf or semidwarf varieties, like IR8 in rice, that responded well to fertilizers in terms
of increased yield without lodging from over-feeding. In addition to yield
potential, other important criteria guided rice breeding, including, in order
of importance, grain quality, growth duration, disease resistance, insect
resistance, drought tolerance, tillering, and cold tolerance. Later releases
such as IR36, R42, and IR64 successively incorporated genetic material
from landraces collected and stored in gene banks or exchanged among
plant breeders to improve resistance and palatability. So successful were

these new varieties that at one point the total area planted to IR36 alone topped eleven million hectares, making it the most widespread rice cultivar on record (Swaminathan 1982). IR 64 was more acceptable to consumers than previous releases because the grains had intermediate amylose content and therefore were more translucent and "slippery" and did not break at milling, qualities possessed by Asian landraces to start with. It has been one of the most popular varieties planted, in the mid-1990s covering as much as eight million hectares (Khush 1995). Successful adoption in the case of IR 36 and IR 64 can, of course, also be read as unfortunate displacement, with farmers abandoning many of the traditional rice varieties they have favored and relied on for generations.

The design-driven breeding approach (Donald 1968; Kropff et al. 1995), coupled with the credit-backed agricultural extension system, has paved the way for the conception of, and support for, a formal ideotype design (see chapter 1). The danger of breeding a rice ideotype that will thrive in both favorable (lowland, irrigated, adjacent or connected to markets) and unfavorable (upland, rain-fed, inaccessible) conditions is the possible surrender of the last marginal repositories of traditional varieties and wild relatives to homogenization. More insidious still, but beyond the scope of this book, is the possibility of reduction of the genetic diversity of the world's important crops through contamination from transgenic introductions. In assessing rice genetic diversity in Asia, Michael Jackson (then director of the International Rice Germplasm Center at IRRI) maintained, "Asian rice varieties show an impressive range of variation in many characters such as plant height, tillering ability, maturity, and size of panicles, among others. Variation in grain characters, such as size, shape, and color, is most useful for distinguishing different varieties. Farmers in Asia continue to grow thousands of different varieties. They may be cultivated for specific traits such as aroma or cooking quality or because of a particular cultural aspect" (1995:267). The question, as I see it, is for how long?

On the more optimistic side, the adoption of high-yielding varieties and genetically engineered ones notwithstanding, some farmers in the Philippines are still holding on to the crop varieties and associated local knowledge that have seen them through good times and bad, at least as part of their farming strategy. Whether one is talking about rice or sweet potatoes, these farmers are motivated by the need to be autonomous, that is, to have at hand, to be able to choose, to not have to ask for permission, and to be free to relish and share a diversity of produce. Obviously, not all crop varieties that farmers keep can qualify as landraces because there is considerable incorporation and loss going on at all times. But the conservation of biodiversity in tin cans, in home gardens and subsistence plots, at the border of commercial plots, at times even *in* commercial plots, smuggled and buried in clumps of recommended or "approved" varieties, tells us that there is an ongoing challenge, a constant pushing back. It is as if farmers—as the ground shifts under their feet due to rapid social, economic, and technological change—are looking for continuity and finding it in crops and technologies that "support life" and "do not go up and down," those that they "know by heart." For the rest of us, and mostly without cost to any of us, they keep the family attic stocked up with options that, like transposable elements, should serve us in good stead if the ground shifts in a direction we have not anticipated, or planned for.

CHAPTER 4

Southern Memories in a Globalizing World

• •

So long as the past and the present are outside one another, knowledge of the past is not much use in the problems of the present. But suppose the past lives on in the present; suppose, though encapsulated in it, and at first sight hidden behind the present's contradictory and more important features, it is still alive and active.

—R. G. Collingwood, *An Autobiography*

Memory believes before knowing remembers.

—William Faulkner, *Light in August*

Religion, family, food, and garden—interwoven through ritual and conviviality—have retained a certain degree of primacy in the American South. And yet, perhaps precisely because of these stabilizing forces, the South in recent years has attracted more than its share of growth and immigration. Coca-Cola, CNN, and Hartsfield-Jackson International are but a few of the most obvious manifestations of this increasing globalization. When these stabilizing and globalizing forces meet, the results can be quite interesting. Collision is not exactly what happens, for it is more of a patient grinding—meshing and subverting going hand-in-hand. As we shall see in the accounts that follow, realignment occurs simultaneously with reentrenchment of tastes and ways, with new elements not as much adopted as they are domesticated. In addition, some pockets remain fascinatingly (or frustratingly, depending on one's perspective) sovereign. This sovereignty is palpable at every level and calls to mind Granny, the Confederate woman in Faulkner's *The Unvanquished* (1938) who defends strict standards of femininity while taking on all of her husband's masculine roles with great verve during the Civil War. Scott's "weapons of the weak" (1985), Taussig's "mimesis and alterity" (1993), and the concept of marginality itself take on a whole new texture and torque in this setting as people resist, deny, redefine, engage, appropriate, and reroute the changes taking place around them.

In this chapter, I try to cover a good bit of this variation and its significance while focusing on life histories of seedsavers and gardeners. But first, let us consider "heirloom," "vintage," or "old-timey" plants in relation to sense of place, where I think they have the greatest bearing. The very fact that these adjectives are used for traditional species and varieties of fruit trees, vegetables, and ornamentals is an indication of the familiarity, affection, and dignity associated with what has been passed down from generation to generation. Signifying not only age but, more importantly, lineage and legacy, heirloom plants are highly prized by many Southerners, whether one is talking about garden peas (Strickland 1998), apple trees (Calhoun 1995), or antique roses (Reddell 1999). Two widely agreed-upon criteria are used to distinguish heirloom plants: first, they have been around for fifty years or longer; and second, they are open-pollinated and can be propagated by saving and sowing seeds from a previous harvest. A third quality, which is not always required, is that they have been passed down, or passed along, a kinship-based or other informal or folk network and thus have existed for an extended period of time outside formal seed systems and breeding circles (DeMuth 1998). The long and intimate history of these seeds makes them perfect vehicles for transporting the sights, smells, and textures as well as emotions, stories, and memories that make for a vibrant sense of place. These connections are not simply esoteric; they are quite critical to transformation and persistence. As Keith Basso noted:

> Places possess a marked capacity for triggering acts of self-reflection, inspiring thoughts about who one presently is, or memories of who one used to be, or musings of who one might become. And that is

not all. Place-based thoughts about the self lead commonly to thoughts of other things—other places, other people, other times, whole networks of associations that ramify unaccountably within the expanding spheres of awareness that they themselves engender. The experience of sensing places, then, is both roundly reciprocal and incorrigibly dynamic. (1996:55)

In a summer internship called "Southern Memories," graduate and undergraduate students from the Southern Seed Legacy Project interviewed farmers and gardeners in an effort to conserve heirloom seeds as well as to document associated local knowledge and practices (Nazarea et al. 1997). The predictable and comforting cadence of chopping collard greens, scooping hominy, stirring sorghum syrup, simmering cowpeas, and baking corn bread sustains a placed identity in the American South. One of the memory bankers, Sandra Crismon, interviewed seedsavers in her native Kentucky. A family friend, Mattie Arnett, recalled, "My parents made sorghum [syrup] every year. That was a must. We used sorghum for so many things. We liked to sweeten with it . . . gingerbread, egg butter, all kinds of gingerbread, different kinds." "Do you have any of those old recipes?" Sandra asked, to which Mattie responded, "In my head." "How do you make egg butter?" Sandra persisted, and Mattie relented, "You use eggs and sorghum, nutmeg. . . . You put about a pint of sorghum to three or four eggs, and get your sorghum boiling in a saucepan. Put your eggs in a bowl, and you get them mixed good, put about a third-cup of milk, and beat the eggs all up good, and gradually stir it in your cooking sorghum, then when it gets done, we like nutmeg. . . ." Mattie's brother, Luther Risner, finished the story for her. "It's good for biscuits," he piped in (fig. 18).

Mattie and Luther were born and raised in Morgan County, in eastern Kentucky, but had since moved to Verona, near Cincinnati. Mattie was eighty-three years old at the time of the interview, and Luther was, according to his sister's estimate, in his late eighties. Referring to fragrant plumgrannies that we had featured in *Seedlink*, the Southern Seed Legacy newsletter, Mattie remarked, "I had some [seeds] in the freezer, we had our own saved from year to year, and they were just so sweet and

Figure 18   Luther Risner and Mattie Arnett, from Verona, Kentucky (photo by Sandra Crismon)

good, but I've gone out of seed. When you get old, you lose a lot of those. And when we talk about these seeds being old, they are old, honey, we grew up with them!" They recalled that back in Morgan County, their family planted sweet corn, one kind called the eight-row corn with white, flat grains that they grew in patches and another kind called Country Gentleman, the sweetest corn that they had ever tasted. Their grandfather had an orchard with around thirty apple and peach trees, which he had purchased when "some guy came through the county with a wagonload of peach trees and apple trees . . . and sold them pretty cheap." They had two kinds of apple that they could remember. One was Grimes Golden, to their knowledge one of the oldest varieties in the United States. The other was York Imperial, also known as "Wagoneer," because it was shaped like "a lopsided wagon wheel that froze on the mud on one side, thick, and thin on the other." The apples from the orchard were "awful hard, but they're awful good keepers . . . had a richer taste [compared to] these apples you get now; they seem like they're watery. They didn't grow them as large then. We will never eat an apple that tastes as good as out of that orchard." They were also fond of a cabbage that their mother grew and stored in an ingenious way:

> She'd raise them big cabbage, and then she'd set them out sometime in July. And what we'd do, we'd go right down beside where they grew and dig a ditch in order to cover them up so they'd be under the top of the ground about that much. And then we'd cover that up good, and the tops, we'd pull them up, and let the roots stick up and the head go down. Did you ever hear of that? It's a funny-looking sight to see a bunch of roots sticking up that far through your garden. And then, we'd put them about that close together, so if one did rot, it wouldn't spread to the other. And the ground would be froze, and my mother would take a notion for cabbage, she'd want cabbage. And she'd send me to the garden with an axe and a big digging hoe, any way to get it out. It had a distinct, sweet flavor to it.

In Verona, they have continued to plant a family heirloom, the salad pea—"a little bunch pea, about that tall, and the bloom is purple." Their mother, Nan Risner, had saved the seeds and distributed them to her neighbors for years and years (for this reason, it is also called the Nan Risner pea). This pea, "a whole lot sweeter than other kinds," had been in their family for as long as they could remember. According to Luther, "My parents, they cooked them in an open kettle, just a few minutes and they were done. Best I can remember, they used an old, black cooking kettle, cast iron, you know. You put a little bacon grease in them. Tastes awful good." At present, Mattie and Luther also grow three kinds of beans, a greasy grit bean that is "striped like the pinto bean, only smaller," a cornfield bean that looks like the same bean but "grows as a vine all over the place," and a white bean with which they "didn't have much luck." They also talked about an "antique bean" called "Hoy Burton," after the woman who shared the seeds with Mattie. According to her, it is not uncommon to have varieties named after the people they came from. They were "the best there ever was. . . . They're prolific, grow in bunches, each a handful right up to the stalk!"

Luther also told Sandra a story about their sister who owned a gristmill and had a habit of grinding more white corn than she and her family could ever use, "a big bunch of meal." She and her husband divided up the white cornmeal and sent it all over the county to people who had never seen it. He gave her some seeds of Hoy Burton beans:

> She's a connoisseur of stuff like that, and she planted them and liked them awful well. She was at a memorial meeting . . . and this man's sister they lived close to complained to her, "I'm troubled, I lost my good bean. My brother's dead now and he gave them to me many, many years ago. I've lost them and I don't know what I'm gonna do. And my sister said, "Honey, don't worry, I got plenty of them. Luther had got them through Hoy, gave them to so and so and so" and it tickled her to death.

It seems seeds in rural Kentucky pass hands, ostensibly disappear, and are found again to everyone's delight. Token seeds or samples of traditional varieties like the meal from white corn, referred to by Mattie and Luther as "good communicators," crisscross among family members, friends, neighbors, rivals, and acquaintances sustained by sensory recollections of tastes, textures, and smells that were "awful good."

While seed exchange among Southern farmers and gardeners tends to be through informal and kinship-based pathways, some seedsavers, such as Fanny Lou Bryan, found success with small-scale commercialization. Fanny Lou prepared and sold cucumber salad from an old-timey cucumber variety that her neighbor had given to her (fig. 19). In one conversation, memory banker Lan Jia and Fanny Lou compared the different uses of cucumber in China (cooked as an ingredient in various dishes) and the United States (eaten raw). Fanny Lou told Lan that her "white cucumber is better than green ones. Really delicate, meat there is real fine, little seed." She further explained:

> I don't have any white cucumber [now], but I got the seeds. I've grown it for years. . . . I eat and don't peel them at all. They're real good cucumber. I've been selling the seeds [since] my husband died in 1979. . . . The lady next door gave them to me, then she died at

Figure 19   Fanny Lou Bryan's white cucumber (photo by Lan Jia)

ninety; that's her mother's cucumber seeds. She gave me some of them. She had a garden there. Somebody said, "Why don't you try to sell it?" I said I don't know if I could or not. They said, "Try, through the 'Market Bulletin.'" I tried. I sell cucumber seed and plumgranny seeds for years now.

Fanny Lou was born on a farm in Lumpkin County, Georgia. She recalled, "We had a lot of things on the farm. We had pumpkins, peas, corn, beans. We grew everything: watermelon, cantaloupes, all that stuff." They also had fragrant plumgrannies or "smell melons," and she re-members them vividly by their fragrance, "fine, sweet, they go rot. . . . It is funny, all the kids had a pocket, you have a pocket to put your pencils in, the kids put plumgrannies in pockets when they were around . . . they said, 'Let me smell your plumgranny, let me smell your plumgranny.'" Her mother passed away when she was nine, and since her father never remarried, she cooked for and practically raised her two brothers and a sister. Before settling in Dahlonega, Georgia, she and her husband had lived in Baltimore, where her husband worked in the shipyard. When her husband died of a drowning accident several years before the interview, she thought she could never make a garden like her husband's. But for three years, before the property was sold, she planted "more stuff [than] you can ever grow in a little garden like that . . . rows of Irish potato, bush potato, sweet potatoes . . . beans, corn, cabbage, broccoli, cauliflower . . . I had everything!"

Now in her seventies, Fanny Lou plants white cucumbers and yellow plumgrannies for home use and for sale. She explained how she saves seeds every year and sells them:

> You can't get seeds when they're little; you have to wait for them to get complete, matured. Then take them out, cut them off from the vines. I put them out, then wash, wash, wash. Take a Tupperware colander, put the seeds in it, rub, rub, rub. You see how clean they are to save them a long time. Then, dry them three to four weeks to get them real, real dry, and then take bags and put them in the 'frigerator. Sold around two hundred dollars [worth] this year. Every year, I sell two hundred to three hundred dollars [worth], save my money, and buy my VCR, microwave. I enjoy that. I sold every year and gave my friend across the street over there. So she grows them there and gives me the seeds. I give her half the money.

Orders come from as far away as California. She attributed the widespread attention to a railway engineer who carried a copy of the *Georgia Farmers and Consumers Market Bulletin* on board his train. The issue evidently made its way across the South and into the West, allowing others on board to spot Fanny's cucumbers and plumgrannies among the ads. The widespread exposure of Fanny Lou's seeds is not at all inconsequential or irrelevant to the subject of the human impact on the conservation of plant genetic resources. The ripple effect of alternatives to the formal seed system can in fact be far-reaching.

Among readers of the *Market Bulletin* was Ernest Keheley, who responded to an ad for seeds of different varieties of cowpeas (fig. 20). The listing had been posted by one of my students, Eleanor Tison. Ernest, then eighty, also responded enthusiastically to our requests for interviews for the Southern Seed Legacy. He regarded the *Market Bulletin* as his comic page because the units of measure used for old-timey seeds ("shotgun box full," "thimbleful") struck him as particularly funny. In addition, he was always amused by the different ways people handled seed exchange, with some insisting on paying for packets of seeds that they requested and others not even offering to cover postage. His usual response to an inquiry about remuneration was, "Why, you don't understand, we'd always be neighbors, we swap! I don't sell seed, they're supposed to be certified to sell 'em. I'll send you all you want, you can pay me for the postage if you want to." Ernest lives less than ten miles from the affluent suburb of Marietta, Georgia, in the original family home, built in 1909. With its rocking-chair porch, tomatoes, cowpeas, gourds, marigolds, and daylilies, the house looks like a vestige of the past in the midst of sparkling new developments. When he sat on his porch, drivers and passengers of every car would wave at him, and he would wave back. When I remarked at how friendly his neighbors seemed, his response was, "I've trained them well." And perhaps he had. Ernest has experienced a lot in life and has traveled across the globe and back.

As he was growing up, Ernest was surrounded by the wheat, corn, cotton, oats, and cowpeas that his father rotated in their farm and the sage, tomatoes, squash, cabbage, cantaloupe, and a rich variety of beans, peas, and cowpeas that his mother grew in her garden. He remembers these days fondly:

> When [my father] and my mother married, they didn't have nothin'. But he had to get up and go to work, and he worked at day labor for them at this big farm. . . . Cut wood, haul rocks, build fences, whatever it was, fine. And he made up, got 'em for nothin' and went up the road and got a piece, they bought a house and a few acres. . . . He liked to garden, but the field come first. The garden was just a pastime, he got it up but whenever we got everything out finally, he said, "Boys, we gonna plant today."

Although Ernest recognized that his parents "didn't have nothin'" as he was growing up, neither scarcity nor drudgery entered his stories. On the contrary, his childhood memories seemed to overflow with abundance

Figure 20   Ernest Keheley carving out
a gourd for a purple martin's nest.
(photo by Eleanor Tison)

and happiness. As Ernest recalled, "When we boys would go out to
plant cotton, we would take some plumgranny seeds with us and plant
them out in the cotton field. We would also take some watermelon seeds
with us and plant them out there. Then later when you'd be pickin'
cotton, you'd come across a watermelon and could sit down to have a
bite. But we never ate the fragrant plumgrannies, just gave them to the
girls."

During World War II, Ernest joined the military and traveled all
over Asia, at some point even attempting to introduce Rutger's tomatoes in India. This venture was hugely unsuccessful, though, as the leaves
and stems just kept growing without actually producing any tomatoes in
India's heat, rainfall, and humidity. When he returned to Georgia, he
resumed his occupation as a tractor mechanic but still pursued gardening avidly and continued to absorb everything. Among his crops, peas
seem to be his favorite, and he keeps several kinds: Blue Goose ("I have

no idea what the real name is, it's been handed down from somebody else, somebody else, somebody else"); Whippoorwill ("a different light brown . . . with great long pods and, if at the right stage, you can shell them easy, and they're easy to pick"); Red Ripper ("taste so good, that's why we keep 'em"); Colossus ("the best darn peas I've ever seen"); Hercules ("it's packed in there, almost stuck together . . . bigger than the end of my thumb, you can fill a pot quick"); and black-eyes ("every time there's a pea, people gonna say it's black-eye"). His collection is a mixture of seeds with different histories—pass-alongs from family and friends that comprised the bulk of his collection because "in the old days, you always know somebody who knows somebody else," seeds he picks up on his trips to old-timey country seed stores that he regularly visits just "to see how 'bout see somethin' I ain't never seen before," and those he occasionally orders from catalogues, which are mostly interesting seeds of plants that are "only somethin' to look at, something odd."

His knowledge comes from equally diverse sources. Experience, for example, has taught him that peas will keep for a long time and see you through winter if you know what you are doing. According to Ernest:

> You wait 'til the hull's dead before you pick it. And then just lay 'em out and spread 'em out and let the sun dry 'em 'til they're real dry. Well, we take those dry peas in winter time, and you have to soak 'em like any other dry beans, and you go to the smokehouse and cut off a big rash of side meat, ham hock, whatever you know, and boil it. Yeah, and make some cracklin' corn bread.

Sharing his insights on seedsaving, he offered, "We did not know anything about seedsaving like people do now, freezing them and all, we just let them dry and kept them in a bag. . . . A friend of mine said he always picks out the longest pods for planting. If you kept the little ones, then you'd have little pods next year and that's no good." In Ernest's view,

> You'll find out that you learn a lot of things . . . you go to school, you'd read books, read technical manuals, [but] some of that ole everyday common sense gotta be thrown in with it. . . . I don't care what you're doing, whether it's farmin', or workin' on machinery, or

anything in life. It's good to have readin' and find out what the tech-nical workings of it is. But you gotta have some common sense.

In suburban Marietta, with its tidy, professionally landscaped lawns, Ernest's gardening common sense provides an arresting visual counter-point, like a mischievous surprise element worked into an otherwise dis-ciplined quilt.

Unlike Ernest, whose home place was threatened by urban growth, Vi Johnson and her husband, Benny, had shared a house surrounded by descendants of the original Gullah-Geechee community of former Afri-can slaves who settled in Hog Hammock on Sapelo Island, Georgia. Ironi-cally, some long-time residents presently feel closed-in, too, not by run-away urban sprawl but by government regulation. Hog Hammock is part of the Sapelo Island National Estuarine Reserve, which means that development on the island is strictly monitored by the state through the Department of Natural Resources. In-migration, construction of addi-tional infrastructure, importation of machinery, and selling of land to outsiders in particular are tightly controlled so as not to overtax the carrying capacity of the reserve. This level of regulation has led to some complaints from the residents of Hog Hammock that they were being squeezed out of existence, the growth of their community frozen. How-ever, the natural and cultural legacy of the island has been preserved, as attested by the giant live oaks draped with Spanish moss, thriving ma-rine life, clean-swept yards fronting houses, elements of kitchens and living rooms conveniently and invitingly located on the yards, overgrown and tangled gardens of cowpeas and beans, comforting familiarity with everybody knowing everybody else, and abundance of common surnames in the old cemetery.

When we first met Vi Johnson, she was minding her store, the "BJ Confectionary," and taking care of her grandson, who stays with her while his parents work on the mainland. Her grandson often has plenty of company, as he is joined by other young ones in watching videos in one corner of the store and exploring the many interesting swimming holes and hiding places on the island. Their parents are nowhere to be seen most days except Sunday. This pattern among the families in Hog

Hammock, of letting young ones stay with their grandparents before they go to school and during summer vacations, maintains close ties between generations despite the physical relocation necessitated by limited work opportunities and settlement prospects for younger generations on the island itself. This is evidenced by the fact that young people who do not stay on the island regularly take the ferry from MacIntosh County on the mainland to Sapelo every Sunday morning, as well as on special occasions, to participate in the lively church service and partake of the picnic of fried chicken, sweet potatoes, beans, and greens with family and friends. They bring in news from the outside and take away supplies of food and, oftentimes, seeds.

Aside from the church, the BJ Confectionary is a popular gathering place on the island where one can always get crunchy dill pickles, pickled pig knuckles, and cold soda, even freshly cooked barbeque when Benny Johnson was still alive. The store has hosted a distinguished parade of visitors to the island, including former president Jimmy Carter, whose photographs covered one wall. My student, Eleanor Tison, went back a couple of times to visit with Vi and interview her about her garden. Like Fanny Lou Bryan, Vi was always watching from the sidelines and participating as an interested apprentice in gardening while she was growing up in her parents' home in Savannah, Georgia, and when she and her husband moved to Sapelo Island and started their own garden. Her mother and father kept a "huge vegetable garden." Vi remembers that her father mainly raised "a lot of watermelon." Most of it was for the family to enjoy, but he also sold some of it. She remembered him breaking up the soil every spring and keeping it weeded through the planting seasons. She helped him with this task, the sensation of pulling out grass from the field still with her. But it was her mother who "grew all kinds of greens . . . collard, mustard, turnip . . . she also had potatoes, tomatoes, okra." Vi's husband, Benny, a native of Sapelo, had a big garden behind their house and another in a fenced side yard between the store and the house.

When Benny passed away, Vi assumed the main role in the garden, but she recruited someone to help her break the ground and confined her activities to the fenced side yard. She just could not keep up a large garden, but what the garden lacked in size, she made up for in terms of

Figure 21 Vi Johnson's grandson examining a cowpea seed collection, Sapelo Island, Georgia (photo by Eleanor Tison)

its diversity. She planted red peas and black-eye peas, turnip greens and collard greens, okra, "white" beans ("same as butterbeans"), eggplants, tomatoes, corn, and bell peppers. She is very fond of her peas because "you have them year round and they grow real easy . . . don't need to add fertilizer or anything to get them to grow . . . oh, yeah I eat them green or dry . . . have them with rice, or plain . . . boiled with a little bacon fat" (fig. 21). Fall planting for her means putting in her favorite greens.

Occasionally, Vi would get some seeds from relatives on the Georgia coast, in Brunswick and Darien, but her main "exchange partner" for vegetable seeds was her neighbor, Allen Green, himself an old-time resident of Sapelo. Allen grows a big patch of peas and is well known around Hog Hammock as the unfailing source of red Seminole pea seeds. Somewhat of a legend on the island for living life on his terms, he is also known as the last person to stop planting rice and making cane syrup. Allen is fond of saying, "I held out. . . . I lasted longer than anyone else," and he still smokes his own hogs and weaves his own baskets. When asked why she continued to garden, Vi smiled broadly and explained, "Oh, I enjoy it. If you've got ground to plant in, I don't see why not. You can grow [your own food] yourself. You can go out and pick what you want and know what's in them. What's in your food, you know, sprays; you never know with store-bought food. I may try beets next year. My parents used to grow beets. My father loved them with onions and vinegar!"

In Clinton, Tennessee, memory banker Katie Price interviewed Helen and Rudolph Humphrey (fig. 22). Both in their seventies, Helen and Rudolph have been farming for most of their lives. Although they have yielded the saving of some seeds and turned to stores and other sources, they still persist in saving their favorites. One example was given by Rudolph:

> We called it Indian corn; it had red grains in it. It was white corn, only once in a while it'd have a red grain, and sometimes you'd get a whole red ear. That was when we shuck corn, we'd have twenty shuckings back when I was a boy, and, of course, somebody would pass the bottle around, too—the older ones. If you found a red ear, you'd get a stick of candy. And you'd sit there and shuck corn until twelve o'clock at night, and they'd throw it out here in the shed, and then you'd find these red grains. Of course, you'd get so many of them counted up. But if you found a whole red ear you got a stick of peppermint candy. Well, back then, peppermint candy tasted pretty good, but somehow I haven't liked it like I used to. But I've tried a little of everything.

The Humphreys save the seeds for their flavor, appearance, and other favored traits as well as for the way they bring back comforting memories of their youth. Rudolph can still recall when, "back a long time ago you had to depend on what you saved or had." Their families and their neighbors planted Honeydrip and a kind of Blue Ribbon sugarcane. He and his brother used to operate a mill and produced three thousand to forty-five hundred gallons of molasses each year. Now, his brother having passed on, Rudolph has given up on the mill. To his

Figure 22 Helen Humphrey,
from Clinton, Tennessee,
showing her favorite cutshort
beans (photo by Katie Price)

knowledge, Honeydrip and Blue Ribbon sugarcane have disappeared,
"You can't find them no more." He complains that "a hog couldn't eat"
the molasses that is available now; today's mill operators "don't get the
skimmings off them, and they take the hide off your throat."

Every spring, Helen and Rudolph sow their Indian corn and a variety of greens and beans. They have also been saving a special kind of
pumpkin seed that they have been growing all their lives:

> Field pumpkins they are. There is two kinds of pumpkin; there's a
> male pumpkin and a female pumpkin. And you probably never knew
> that, and your books didn't tell you that either. Your female pumpkin
> has got a big blossom end on it, and your male pumpkin has got a
> little bitty blossom on it, and if you don't mix them seeds together,
> you won't raise no pumpkins. . . . You can't buy these no more because

you don't buy old field pumpkins no more. No company has them. We used to call them Kentucky field pumpkins, but you can't even get them out of Kentucky no more. . . . Anyway, we've had them. They all got big and round. You could have walked about a half-acre and never walked on the ground. I mean they was just about laying-a-touching!

They reminisced about other edible garden crops like the "turkey bean" that got its name from the way it originated from three seeds found in the craw of a wild turkey when it was killed. Rudolph did not care much for beans and greens (he seemed to think, or his mother had warned him, that they were only for women), and so Helen took care of most of the garden after he plowed the soil and worked it up. According to Helen, she "just doesn't fool with" certain plants, like squash, while she gives a lot of care and attention to others:

> I've got a few old-fashioned beans. Cutshorts, I save me some of them. Well, I like them peanut beans [another name for cutshorts]; if I had to make just one type of beans, [they] would be my favorite. My peanut beans: used to save them but it's got to where you can buy them now. I've [also] got them turkey beans; I save some of them seeds, and I planted two rows out there in the corn. My first ones didn't do too well this year, but I've planted them cutshorts, and I've picked a couple of times off them.

The Humphreys also grow Brown Bunch beans, an early-maturing variety that, according to Rudolph, "You couldn't wait until they had beans in them if you were going to eat them because they'd be tough hulls." Helen expressed her consternation at how some of their old favorites seemed to have slipped through their fingers. She lamented that Rudolph couldn't make hominy from "that old-timey cane" anymore. "You can't save Hickory cane for seed anymore because it's hybrid."

In a less than perfect world, everything is subject to compromise, even specifications of memory. One plants a traditional garden using a mixture of saved and store-bought seeds. One re-creates a dish that holds a lot of meaning but uses an ingredient from a hybrid instead of an old-timey variety. Yet, as Ernest has prescribed, and as Helen and Rudolph are obviously practicing, seedsavers try a little bit of everything, throw in a lot of common sense, and craft a not-so-rigid perspective and a creative strategy that somehow approximate and satisfy their preferences. It could be in the form of seedsaving and exchange for pleasure, as in the case of Mattie and Luther; or it could be in the form of a seed flow with a little cash incentive, as Fanny Lou has been practicing. With a sense of creativity, adventure, and contingency in their passions and pursuits, Southern seedsavers make us pause and reconsider: Is homogenization all that necessary? Is globalization all that inescapable?

No logical matrix can be drawn, no predictive statements ventured, because recollections, descriptions, and preferences slice constrained reality every which way, and what stands out in the end is the fact that there is no wholesale surrender and loss, only active remembering and negotiated "common sense choices." What we do know is that interest in plants with a past—or, if you will, plants with a pedigree—is growing, not diminishing. Thus, while the 1994 *Garden Seed Inventory* noted that two-thirds of the five thousand nonhybrid varieties available in 1984 had disappeared from the pages of seed catalogues in one decade (DeMuth 1998), a growing interest in heirlooms had spawned at least twelve seedsaving books, nine specialty seed companies, twelve dedicated Web sites, and six grassroots networks in the same time span (Barnes and Gray 2004). The 1972 National Academy of Sciences Report noted that one variety of sweet potato accounted for 96 percent of acreage devoted to the crop; 76 percent of the bean crop was made up of only three varieties; and virtually the whole pea crop was comprised of just two varieties. Yet we have seen in gardens of Southern seedsavers a wealth of named varieties of all three, each with its own set of origin stories, family anecdotes, and special uses. Carolyn Jabs, in a wonderful book called *The Heirloom Gardener*, put it this way:

> Some gardeners will grow the old variety because they believe they are genuinely better than modern varieties; some will grow them just to perpetuate their genes just so they will be available for future use. Either way, heirloom gardeners are part of the self-reliant American tradition of pitching in to save a heritage of choice and freedom.

Caught between the past, which often seems quaint but irrelevant, and the future, which bears down on us with unseemly speed, many of us grope for something that we can accept from our ancestors and pass on to our children without apology. For more and more gardeners, heirloom seeds are just such inheritance. (1984:18)

These developments are by no means confined to the South—two of the most successful projects in the country are the Seedsavers Exchange, operating in the Midwest; and Native Seeds/SEARCH, based in the Southwest. They clearly indicate a resurgence of seedsaving and old-timey gardening despite the pressures of modern existence. It seems to me that these pressures only serve to intensify the motivation to restore an endangered sense of place. In many instances, heirloom plants play a central role in the restoration of landscapes of remembrance. Some of the reasons for the resurgence of interest in garden staples from another time are distinct flavor, beauty, aroma, novelty and whimsy, evocativeness and familiarity, carefree productivity, and drought and insect tolerance.

For the present generation of small-scale, low-input farmers and gardeners, heirloom plants appeal to wider philosophical inclinations that emphasize harmony and sustainability, including new-age ethical and environmental concerns. Gardening with these folk varieties provides a much-needed connection to nature—a *placed nature* or, as Kant would say, "Nature made specific." The practice forges a link as well to the community and to the past for young people who, engulfed in a modern malaise of "placelessness," are questioning the fast-paced, excessive, and disposable lifestyle they have inherited. The same goes for burned-out "baby boomers" who desire more than anything to downsize and slow down. It must not be forgotten, however, that this resurgence of interest and pride, a social movement built upon an enlivening of the senses and a contagion of emotion, is only possible because the seeds have been kept and passed on by unaffiliated seedsavers who took a liking to these old-timey plants and patiently nurtured them in their small plots of land.

CHAPTER 5

Out-of-Place
Sense of Place

• •

Improperly contextualized, the stories of ordinary people [from the past] stand in danger of remaining just that: stories. To become something more, the partial, "hidden histories" have to be situated in the wider worlds of power and meaning that gave them life.

—Comaroff and Comaroff, *Modernity and Its Malcontents*

In secret places, far from pomp and pride,
The kind affections of the soul abide.

—Park Benjamin, unpublished poem

If seeds and memories are important to people who are rooted in place like the heirloom farmers and gardeners of the American South, how critical are these "resources" to people who have uprooted from their place of origin and settled in a foreign land or, for that matter, who perpetually negotiate two worlds, never completely belonging to one or the other? The domestication of an alien landscape must be one of the greatest challenges to human fortitude and imagination. Two simultaneous stresses impinge on one's consciousness daily—the need to reshape one's environment, and the need to reshape oneself. In *The Senses Still*, Seremetakis remarked that, in popular English usage, nostalgia has been reduced to a sort of "trivializing romantic sentimentality" (1994:4). She contrasted this modern notion to the Greek composite term *nostalghia*, which means desiring with burning pain (noun, *algho*) to journey back (verb, *nosto*) to the homeland. She argued that "nostalgia, in the American sense, freezes the past in such a manner as to preclude it from any capacity for social transformation in the present, preventing the present from establishing a dynamic perceptual relationship to its history. Whereas the Greek etymology evokes the transformative impact of the past as unreconciled historical experience" (1994:4).

What creative responses are available to those for whom nostalgia remains "a burning desire," "an ache to journey back" in space and time? Barbara McClintock would tell us that such turbulence of pain is bound to fire off an unprogrammed response from some deep, in this case, cultural-psychological or spiritual recesses, while Ernest Bloch would remind us that hope is perpetually nurtured in a "wish landscape" that at any moment threatens to congeal (see chapter 2). Although nostalgia and hope have not figured prominently in recent assimilation-versus-transnationalism debates, I would argue that these feelings comprise a haunting cognitive-emotional-sensory field that is highly relevant. The transnationalism position maintains that contemporary immigrants prioritize linkages to their homelands and social networks among compatriots over establishing firm ties in their host countries (Appadurai 1991; Kearney 1995). Rather than striving for assimilation, many immigrants pursue a more fluid, border-straddling existence (Glick-Schiller et al. 1992; Levitt 2001). The main irony, as pointed out by Nagel, is that "to become 'the same' or 'one of us' requires innumerable acts of conformity and accommodation through which immigrants [and other minorities] position themselves in dominant spaces and spheres, often in the face of exclusion and marginalization" (2002:928). How is a sense of place established when one is undeniably, irreparably, "out of place"?

In the lives of immigrants, we see some answers. Here I focus on gardening and seedsaving, particularly of plants from the homeland, as quiet but deeply gratifying acts of connection and emplacement. In contrast to remittances, investment capital, and votes that are often used as measures to track linkages of immigrants to their home countries (Itzigsohn 1999), seeds travel in the opposite direction and *grow* in the host country as living, tangible units, not of capital, but of remembrance. These seeds sprout in plots and fringes that nurture an incredible variety of

edible, medicinal, ceremonial, and ornamental plants—sacred spaces that
are carved out of foreign, urban, transient, and sometimes hostile landscapes. The actual physical location hardly matters. It is as if for the
respective seedsavers, the gardens serve to secure one's place and vali-
date one's existence: I garden, therefore I am. To drink from these gardens is to quench one's longing and appease one's pain.

For the past two years, we have been undertaking a research called
"Introduced Germplasm from Vietnam: Documentation, Acquisition,
and Preservation" as a first step in studying and conserving contributions to plant genetic diversity from different immigrant groups in the
United States. As with our other research projects, our overarching goal
was to document and conserve genetic diversity in the context of cultural
diversity, a particularly urgent task when it comes to second-generation
immigrants for whom the pressure to assimilate can be rather oppressive
and disorienting. Toward this end, we recruited students of Vietnamese
descent to work with us in conserving seeds and other planting materials of Vietnamese vegetables, fruits, herbs, and ornamentals and to document the uses and beliefs associated with these plants in the gardening,
cooking, healing, and ceremonial practices of the older generation of
Vietnamese in America, all of them original immigrants. It should be
noted, briefly, that South Vietnamese refugees first came to the United
States in 1975, followed by a second wave in 1980 and subsequent migra-
tions thereafter. Approximately one million reside in the United States
today, concentrated in large metropolitan and semitropical areas such as
California, Louisiana, and Florida, where they have integrated but at the
same time held on to much of their foodways. Although many studies
have been conducted on their resettlement, acculturation, and role transformations, little research has been done on their gardening philosophies
and practices or on their contribution to the agricultural diversity of their
adopted country (Airries and Clawson 1994; Rhoades and Nazarea 2003).

The younger generation of Vietnamese Americans still know and
appreciate Vietnamese food, although they may not prepare such dishes
on a regular basis when living on their own. They recognize many plants
from Vietnam, although they can't always identify them by name. Some
wonder why their parents persist in cultivating a diversity of Vietnamese

plants in their new home, especially since most of the edible ones can easily be procured from Vietnamese or Asian grocery stores. For many of the student participants, the memory banking research marked the first opportunity to talk to their parents and elders more than casually about the lives they left behind in Vietnam and their feelings about coming to the United States. For instance, our research assistant for the Vietnamese Germplasm Project, Kathy Nhan Couch, twenty-three years old, asked her mother, Nhan Nguyen Couch, why she wanted to come to the United States in 1975 when she was herself barely twenty-three. Her mother replied, "I don't want to come here—I have to. . . . I leave the country because at that time I married an American so I have a son. The communists came, and I heard the communists don't like Americans at that time, so I can't stay there because my son was half-American."

Since 1975, when she first arrived, Nhan has lived in Marietta, Georgia, moved to North Carolina, and returned to Georgia, where she has "been stuck, until now," in Columbus. She worked as a waitress in a bar before she could familiarize herself with dimes and quarters, and she learned to order beer for her customers by signaling with her fingers before she could speak English:

> I can count money but I didn't know they called [them] quarters, dimes, and nickels. In Vietnam, my daddy's mama had a country store and sold beer but only two different kinds of beer over there. . . . At first I started working here and they had too many beers and my English not good. So good thing the music was so loud. . . . They teach you how to put your fingers up. . . . So you really talked by your hands because the music was so loud.

Later, she became a cocktail waitress at Fort Benning. Without knowing how to name or mix drinks, she made mistakes she had to pay for dearly. Laughing and shaking her head, she explained, "When the customer said that wasn't what they ordered, I'd dump it out and make another one. When I go to work, I had ten dollars. When I come home, I had five dollars," But whether it was dimes and quarters, beer or cocktail drinks, "It was funny learning. . . . I needed a job, and I learned quick."

Learning, and learning "quick," comes easily to Nhan. As a little girl in Vietnam, she lived in a "real country county" called Vinh Long. Bananas, coconuts, tangerines, mango, bamboo, kapok—"all kinds of trees"—grew around their house. Their property was not very big, but there was always a lot of food. Her mother kept a country store and was also a good cook who was often called upon to prepare traditional Vietnamese fare and French cuisine at weddings and other special occasions. Her father was a taxi-bicycle driver and a seasoned carpenter who knew a lot about choosing and preserving wood. There was a small, one-room private school near her home, but the public school was some fifteen miles away across the river. Her parents could not afford to enroll her in the private school, and, after trying for a few months, she found it was just too difficult to walk to the distant public school every day. So she learned to read while playing and paying attention outside the private school on her "off" days.

Before her parents discovered that she had dropped out of the public school, Nhan had filled up all of her mother's containers of rice outside their house. This was because she got into the habit of setting out at dawn every morning pretending to go to school when in fact she spent most of the day gleaning rice grains from the discarded stalks that had been left in the fields by the harvesters. After she was found out (and duly castigated), she started scaling up her entrepreneurial ventures. When she was eight or nine, she gathered bananas, coconut, and fruits from neighbors' yards ("there was a lot and they didn't mind") and large leaves that grew wild on the river ("like elephant ears—people wrapped pickled fish in those leaves") and sold them every morning in the market of Can Tho across the river. She also sold water lily roots, which people ate, and leaves of *tao cao*, which older people rolled and chewed with tobacco leaves. After she stripped the leaves, she made brooms of their spines, also to sell. By the time she was eleven or twelve, she had enough capital to have a flourishing rice cake business:

> There was a lady who lived about three houses down. She made cakes to sell, too. I didn't know how to do it, but I go to see her, and I'd watch her to see how to make it. Finally I learned. But before I

learned how to crack the coconuts, I had to bring over the coconut, knife, and bowl to her house so she could crack it for me. From her, I learned how to make one hundred a day. . . . I do real good. My cakes sold real quick. I learned to make more . . . two hundred a day, the most I made was 330 a day. So everyday I left home about three in the morning and go to the river. The boat driver picked me up every morning. I made 330 rice cakes, half the rice cakes with banana inside it, the other half with mung beans.

She saved her money and bought dishes and table utensils for her household:

See, in Vietnam, we had family reunions, or when a family member dies, every year they have a family reunion. . . . When I was little I said, "One of these days, I'd like to buy all the dishes so if my family has a reunion they don't have to borrow from somebody." So every time I made some money, I'd buy a little bit almost everyday . . . two or three dishes, two or three forks or spoons.

She maintained this philosophy even after she moved to the United States, except she applied it to houses. She lived in a mobile home in 1975, bought her first house ("very small, less than one thousand square feet") in 1976, bought her second house and rented out her first in 1980 and from then on, "Every time I saved a couple of thousand dollars, I called a real estate agent and said I would buy a house if someone would finance it for me." She would work on the houses, remodel them and paint them herself (with Kathy and her brother in tow when they were not in school), and then she would rent them out. In the process, she mastered enough skills to be able to make a living repairing other people's houses. She also attended a real estate course at Columbus College, knowing she could not get a license because she had no high school diploma ("I took it anyway to learn what I can. I wanted to learn what the law is"). She put down two thousand dollars for her third house and lives in a fourth—an old one that was moved to the country to make way for a parking lot. Asked how she liked living in the country, she replied:

To me, it doesn't matter where I live. I like to have a little garden. If somebody calls me to do repairs, I go to work on it right away, if I have to, the same day. If not, then I stay at home. I like to stay at home. I want to keep my yard and plant some flowers, some vegetables. You'll never eat all you plant anyways, so I like to plant a little of everything, just to look at and go out there and water. Most vegetables I give away because I cannot eat it all. . . . Most time I plant something you cannot buy. Just like yard-long beans, but yard-long beans don't last long. Sometimes in a week or two it will be all over, and so I try to plant them one or two weeks apart. When one is over we have another one ready to eat. I'm bad about it. Sometimes at two or three in the morning I like to cook something to eat. I go and pick it from the garden, some vegetables like mint or onion. Sometimes friends come over and have fun and eat.

Although she was not able to bring any seeds from Vietnam when she came to the United States, there is no dearth of seeds and other planting materials from friends who go back to Vietnam or from Asian grocery stores. She once received seeds of sweet corn, called "*bat*" in Vietnam, from a friend. She planted the seeds in her garden and, at ten feet tall, the corn plants were very different from the modern American variety. Vietnamese sweet potatoes are also different; according to Nhan, they are "dry and a different kind of sweet . . . white ones with purple skin and purple in the middle too." Not surprisingly, her present collection attracts a good deal of attention from neighbors and people who are just passing by in Columbus:

> I have long, green squashes [*bau*]—I think they call them gourds here—lemon grass and chives from Vietnam, little purple onions, bitter melon, and Vietnamese mustard greens. They're big, look like cabbage, and we make pickle out of that. We have lettuce with thin leaves, not like heads of lettuce here. . . . A lot of times I work outside. . . . I [also] like to go out there and drink my coffee and feed the fish in the morning time. . . . A lot of people came in to talk, talk about my banana trees and vegetables. Sometimes I dig up my banana

Figure 23 Nhan Nguyen
Couch's whimsical garden
composition with chickens
and yard-long beans,
Columbus, Georgia (photo by
Kathy Couch)

tree and give it to them. They want to plant. They say they've never
seen big banana trees like I have.

Nhan Nguyen Couch has surrounded herself with plants she is familiar with, plants that bring her comfort and make her happy and full,
plants that, in effect, enable her to reconstruct the homeland she left
behind (fig. 23). She dreams of moving farther south to Florida so that
she can have Vietnamese fruit and ornamental trees, which cannot survive the Georgia winter. She has a friend who told her that one can grow
lychee trees and sugarcane in Florida. This dream, of moving farther
south to plant familiar trees with sweet fruits or fragrant blossoms is one
that was shared by many Vietnamese gardeners. For them plants are
central to the reconstruction of a beloved but inaccessible landscape.

Thanh Nguyen is a sixty-one-year-old political refugee residing in

Figure 24 Thanh and Tu
Nguyen's meditative lotus
pond, Atlanta, Georgia (photo
by Kathy Couch)

Atlanta, Georgia. Unlike Nhan, his interest in plants and gardening is a
new-found passion. While Thanh and his family live in a typical suburban
ranch house, two aspects were rather striking about the Nguyens' place.
One was the living room, where the yellow and red flag of the former
Republic of Vietnam, a photograph of the Vietnamese emperor who drove
away the Chinese invaders, and another of the five generals of the former
republic who killed themselves after their defeat at the hands of the Communists were prominently displayed. There was also a photograph of
the Binh Hoa Memorial, which is believed to have been bombed by the
Communists. Apart from the patriotic memorabilia, there were more personal items, including a Buddhist shrine to family ancestors and a photograph of Thanh and his wife, Tu Huyn, in front of the first house they
owned in the United States, adorned with a vase of lucky bamboo. Outside,
in the garden, Thanh had created a rock sculpture in the shape of Vietnam, close to a small pond and bench where he took his afternoon nap

(fig. 24). He and his wife planted Vietnamese vegetables, flowers, and herbs in a neat, trellised garden nearby.

Thanh comes from a big family in Vietnam. He had one older brother and six younger sisters. His parents farmed about ten acres, growing rice, watermelon, and some vegetables. He himself never worked much on the farm because his parents wanted him to get an education. According to Thanh, there was "no reason" for him to farm or to garden back in his country. He graduated from the military academy at Dak Lak, and at twenty-three joined the Twenty-Second Division Infantry. He was in the Ninth Division when he fought with the Vietnamese military against the Communists. According to Thanh:

> [You] cannot compare war with after war. Because before war, it's war everyday. And after war, it's war big time. So many, many trouble before war, because Communists and Republic fighting everyday. So, some economic trouble. But agriculture tax very little bit then. Right now, agriculture tax so high, and [for] Communist people, it's easy [to make a] living. And many, many people, agriculture people, have only little.

Many things changed after 1975. Thanh was imprisoned for nearly ten years, from 1975 to 1984, for his military involvement. He was transferred from one prison camp to another, and his family lost all contact with him until 1979, when his wife finally visited him after learning about his location in North Vietnam. In the meantime, his wife, a high school teacher, had been dismissed from her job and sent to a "reeducation camp" where all educated people were sent. She had to learn about communism six days a week and work on Sundays. She earned a living by whatever means was available to her, including buying and selling sandals in the market. In prison, Thanh learned what it means to be "very, very hungry" and to lose all freedom. As he related, "When the Communists came, you really have to watch what you say. You can't just speak freely about whatever. . . . If you speak against them, somebody is gonna tell the government and they come and arrest you." Prisoners worked outside—planting corn, sweet potatoes, and vegetables—unless they were dizzy or sick, in which case they were sent inside to do some cleaning and "wiping around." Mostly, they were fed meager rations of sweet potatoes and soup, a lot of water, and some vegetables because the prison guards and the kitchen crew ate first. After his release—a development he attributes to increasing international political pressure—he and his family came to the United States. He tries not to let the cold weather in winter and the thin red Georgia soil bother him because, in his words, "I love freedom." He still has a brother and a sister in Vietnam, as well an ageing mother, whom he misses "very much," but he said he is not going back as long as the Communists still rule his country.

Although they did not have much gardening experience in Vietnam, Thanh and Tu started gardening as soon as they acquired their own home in the United States in 1996. They have acquired the seeds of their favorite herbs and vegetables through seed stores and their own social networks. Gardening is their most powerful link to all that was familiar and precious to them. They did not leave with seeds, but in exile they certainly found them. Tu dries and keeps the seeds from one planting season to another, putting them under the sun and keeping them in a dry place in paper bags. They also share their seeds and abundant produce with friends, both Vietnamese and American. Thanh dreams of planting fragrant flowering trees like *cuon gip* and *biu dan* but realizes they cannot survive in Georgia, so they grow what they can. They have also learned to amend Georgia red clay with "lots and lots of topsoil." They now have *bu qua* (bitter melon), some hot peppers, *rau ma* (pennywort), *dua-leo* (cucumber), *dua gang* (similar to watermelon), and aromatic herbs used to flavor meats and soups, like the traditional Vietnamese noodle soup, *pho*. A meditative flowering lotus, *sen*, also adorns their garden. The Nguyens' house and garden seem to be an improvised, evolving memorial to the Vietnam that Thanh and Tu loved and lost and are hoping to see again someday.

An immigrant of a different sort, Don Jose Valverde, can travel quite easily from his place in Nanegal, Ecuador, to his native Colombia. We encountered Don Jose in our research project "Ethnoecology of Fragile Lands in the Andes." Having decided to approach the problem from local people's interpretations of land use change and their relation to biodiversity (Rhoades et al. 2001; Piniero 2002), we had devised several methods to investigate people's perceptions, including story completion test and memory banking. We were interviewing some Nanegal residents in front of one of the two village stores one day when we met Don Jose. Ebullient, and just a little drunk at midday, he approached us and warmly invited us to visit with him. He farmed on frontier land without a legal title (fig. 25). As a result, he was having trouble with the nearby ecological reserve that was intent on expanding and laying down a system of biological corridors and thus was exerting pressure from every conceivable direction to "buy" his land from him. Recently, they had dispatched his son, a security guard in the reserve, to ask him to leave. But for Don Jose, farming was his life, Nanegal was his home, and moving again was out of the question.

Don Jose was known in the community as "the tongue" because he loved telling stories and had a theory on nearly everything. In Colombia, he planted tomatoes, potatoes, barley, and wheat, while in Nanegal he cultivated corn, beans, tomatoes, and potatoes in his farm for the market, and pepper, watermelon, lettuce, and cilantro around the house for food. In the thirty-five years that he has lived and farmed in Nanegal, he has observed many changes, particularly regarding the productivity of the soil:

> Before, the land was new, and everything that was planted was good and produced well; but now the land has run out too, gotten tired. Now, everything needs fertilizer, chemical "remedies" that are expensive. . . . The land is finished, the plants are very weak, but if you give them a handful of fertilizer a month the crops grow well. But the bill just grows and grows! The land won't do anything now, the sugarcane finishes the land and leaves it sterile. The plantanos (plantains) and camotes (sweet potatoes) help the land, though . . . and we are putting chicken manure . . . and with that everything grows.

Don Jose never took things on faith; he tested everything. While his land was mainly devoted to production of vegetables and fruits for consumption and for the market, he devoted certain sections to experimentation. He collected different kinds of seeds and planting materials, which

Figure 25 Don Jose Valverde dipping into his bag of seeds, Nanegal, Ecuador (photo by Robert Rhoades)

he then grew on his farm just to see how they would turn out. He has been disappointed a few times and, consequently, is sometimes given to despair. "We are now *fregados* [hopeless, in bad shape]," he sighed, mainly because of the rapid changes that he cannot control or comprehend. For example, he lamented:

> They now put three quintales [one quintal is approximately equivalent to one hundred pounds] of fertilizer for one quintal of potatoes so, sure, if you see a small piece of land, there is nowhere to step between the plants. It is full of plants because they give them pure ingredients, nutrients for the flowers, for the roots, and so on. It is also because of this that they say all the sicknesses are coming to us and attacking our bodies. . . . The seeds, too, are always changing, like the potato. When the potato gets tired, they plant another potato. They send us certified seeds from Bogotá. These are planted for two seasons, then another kind for two seasons. It always changes.

But if you plant the same potato, it will run out; so you have to keep changing.

Don Jose has come up with his own way of handling his dilemma. When we visited him, his home looked like a typical house on the mountainside—with the requisite calendar, posters from glossy maga-zines, a shrine to a favorite saint, and pictures and certificates honoring grown-up children who had moved to the city. But this impression of conventionality quickly dissipated when Don Jose began pulling out small, crushed paper and plastic bags containing multicolored and variously shaped seeds from the beams on the ceiling, from under chairs and tables, from rough terra-cotta vessels stacked in one corner of the room, and from every step and structural support of the house itself. As he reflected on his inventory:

> At this very moment, I have some beans—victabas, cargabello, bolon rojo—this one is kind of round, and you have to put it in a good spot because it vines and produces in great quantities, and in Colom-bia it is expensive—calima, and orive. I also have nabo castilla, melon, watermelon—need to save them as of this time because their plant-ing season is not 'til April—peas, sambo—pumpkin-type squash, called calabaza in Colombia—zapallo, broccoli, thick-cob corn, thin-cob corn, business corn—typical kind of corn to sell in the mar-ket—cabbage, peppers, tomatoes, potatoes, papaya.

He had brought some seeds from Colombia with him when he moved to Ecuador, while others were acquired from friends and acquaintances over the years. According to him, "The saved seeds have to be cured; you have to put this pink powder with them, make them real dry to protect them or else they will be attacked by pests.' I have been saving seeds for so long . . . to plant when I want to. I can just grab a pouch and plant it when I need to." It seemed that the bags of seeds and the odd combina-tion of plants lovingly tended in his backyard and on his farm gave Don Jose not just pleasure but also a sense of substance and permanence in a tenuous, treacherous world.

In a highly imaginative work, *Surveying the Interior*, Rick van Noy

(2003) examined the writings of surveyors on the landscapes they confront and map. He distinguished the exterior landscape (something out there, blank) from the interior landscape (something in here, felt) and looked at the way that surveyors begin from a predominantly scientific/cartographic vantage point but end up touched by the landscape in multiple ways. Further, van Noy asserts:

> Today, there is hardly a square foot of American landscape that has not been surveyed, digitized, and made readily available on the Internet. But there are still places where one can stand and imagine how wonderfully sublime it must have seemed to early surveyors, and still does. But whereas early explorers navigated by way of rivers, mountains, and other landmarks, today global positioning systems (GPS) can accurately determine location—longitude, latitude, altitude—of people and places almost instantaneously. Technology is also introducing new ways to chart human places, with new kinds of surveyors creating precise three-dimensional maps of the earth and geneticists mapping the human genome. . . . They focus on one sort of knowledge at the expense of other perspectives, such as other ways of knowing the human interior (2003:184).

For immigrants, the process of confronting an unfamiliar landscape must be an approximation of the surveyors' experience, except in a more heightened and immediate sense. They do not confront it with disciplined neutrality and objectivity, nor with technology. They come, instead, with mapped memories that are cognitively and sensorially salient (following Seremetakis, even burning), and it is this *landscape of the interior* that they re-member and re-place on foreign soil. Thus, their gardens are not only physically layered through furrows, hills, and trellises meant to maximize the use of sunlight and space. They are layered emotionally, a reconciliation of the transient nature of their engagement. Another way to think of their gardens is that they are storied and authored; indeed, they are very personal spaces. When one considers how everything changes radically at the moment of relocation, including economic status, societal norms, and generational and gender role expectations, and that immigrants are expected to assimilate yet at every turn are marginalized, it is easy to appreciate how crucial this authoring of place is. As immigrants face a future cast in uncertain terms, the garden provides both anchor and sail.

Transnationalism studies have dwelt on the bordering character of immigrant existence but have not paid much attention to the effect of this "living in two worlds" for the receiving populations. When Nhan's neighbors in Columbus, Georgia, gape at the spreading banana and towering corn plants in her yard and request planting materials, when Thanh and Tu share fresh produce and carefully saved seeds with their American friends, when Don Jose regales mere acquaintances and regular fans with his homespun philosophies and multicolored seeds, what must these concrete moments of aesthetic challenge instill and provoke in the recipients? Would they simply thrill to the novelty and be grateful for the diversion, or would some form of "anticipatory illumination . . . [that] gives rise to hope within the cultural heritage" (Zipes 1988:xxiii) take shape? Might the concrete possibility of melding and straddling two worlds—understandably a scary prospect—actually set in motion lively, creolized ways of personally and collectively transforming hegemonic landscapes?

Whether lived in place or elaborated out of place, a sense of negotiating boundaries and finding openings in novel and spirited ways seems to permeate the stories of seedsavers. Each life trajectory, and therefore each life history, is unique, but stories of non-conformity, recalcitrant behavior, and individual experimentation are not unique to our field sites. Regardless of geographical location, marginal areas provide spaces wherein dominant discourse and policy are contested in thought as well as in practice. In Sierra Leone, for example, Paul Richards (1986) observed more than seventy named varieties of rice that farmers carefully evaluated and either selected or culled based on length of maturity and adaptability to different soil and water conditions. Other criteria that influenced farmer selection were color and milling quality and palatability of grains and, interestingly, individual farmer's fancy. They cultivated *Oryza sativa* and *Oryza glaberrima* and differentiated them from sympatric wild relatives such as *Oryza longistaminata* and *Oryza breveligulata*. Richards found that government agencies liked to promote the most profitable cultivars by restricting the range of available planting materials:

> [But] this policy is not necessarily shared by the villagers. Farmers are as keenly interested in variability as in varietal stability. The belief that it is the nature of the planting material to change over time is widely held and deeply ingrained in social as well as farming practices. Rices are rogued as much to provide interesting new materials after a misfortune as to gamble one's way. Who is to say that they are wrong? In these circumstances, hyper-variability among rices is invested with a rich cultural significance. (1986:176)

Among swidden agriculturalists in northeastern Brazil, creativity is not a deviance but the norm, as evidenced by the fact that "every household's configuration of land types, and crop mix within them, is unique to that household" (Johnson 1972:152). One old man devoted a small portion of his field to the cultivation, and careful observation, of a new strain of manioc he had received from a faraway friend; another farmer separated two strains of rice that are normally planted together to check if they needed distinct management practices. Upon examining an extensive breadth of literature in anthropology, Allen Johnson concluded, "It is inaccurate to depict the traditional agriculturalists in a passive light, programmed by cultural learning to respond to a discrete set of environmental variables in such a way as to maximize his long-term gain. The traditional agriculturalist subsists not merely in a complex environment, he contributes much of that complexity through his own labors" (1972:153). Particularly intriguing is the case of an Iban woman who deliberately selected and saved poorly developed panicles of rice seeds because she took pity on them for being so small and imperfect. Johnson referred to these instances as physical manifestations of "dissident opinion," following Donald Campbell, who wrote, "Dissident opinion, unexpressed while majority opinion is successful, represents a latent potentiality for change if group failure is encountered" (1965:42).

In heirloom plants and folk varieties, we find "artifacts laden with perceptual recall" (Seremetakis 1994:10). Their persistence against the hegemony of modernity sustains stirrings of nostalgia, making the de-

sire to journey back, or to re-create a place, less of a romantic anachronism and more of a real possibility, perhaps even a sensible one. It is
important, in this regard, that seeds and plants are not only distinct and
tangible, but also portable; they can be treasured and hidden, or displayed and exchanged. Given the sea of changes that modernity engenders, everyone suffers a certain degree of placelessness, of abandoning
and abandonment. The response of seedsavers to this double alienation
is to surround themselves with loops of intimacy and comfort. In this
highly creative response, seeds and memories can be kept close and—in
mutual reinforcement—celebrated, shared, and multiplied. If we think
about it, one could do worse, much worse.

   Abraham Heschel (1965) could have been referring to seedsavers
when he wrote, "A human behavior pattern is not a monument to a life
that is gone, but a drama full of life. It is *a system as well as a groping*, a
wavering, a striking forth; solidity as well as outburst, deviation, incon-
sistency; not a final order but a process, conditioned, manipulated, questioned, challenged" (1965:9–10, emphasis added). Their life histories
comprise an interesting commentary on the times—*history writ small*—
but they are also a testimony to the innumerable ways humans deal
creatively with threats of diminishment. The extremes of modernization and commercialization present one such threat, and these farmers
and gardeners have fashioned their own response—"a system as well as
a groping" in the old-timey seeds they save, transport, pass along, and
nurture in their highly varied but always intimate landscapes. But, as
those concerned with potentials for macro transformations may ask, does
the groping ever become a system? Can there ever be collective action or
a staunch science emanating from individual quirks? Or does history
writ small end up being just that? I would argue that it is ultimately out
of individual stories and vernacular visions that histories are made,
whether historians (and scientists) are comfortable with it or not.

CHAPTER 6

Stories and Histories

• •

INTERVIEWER: "Try to explain to me what a tree is."
SUBJECT: "Why should I? Everyone knows what a tree is, they don't need me telling them."
—A. R. Luria, *Cognitive Development: Its Cultural and Social Foundations*

A terror which threatens us all, that of being judged by a power
Which wants to hear only the language it lends us.
—Roland Barthes, *Dominici, or the Triumph of Literature*

In chapters 3, 4, and 5, I discussed the life histories of small-scale farmers and gardeners who, rooted in place or rooting out of place, have nurtured biodiversity through the plants they collect and cultivate. I have tried to make the argument that these plants are cherished and passed along through a sense of curiosity, adventure, fancy, delight, irreverence, and memory and that their presence in unpredictable patches and mosaics creates an effective and persistent deterrent to wholesale biodiversity loss. Like the lone survivor tree that provides a haven and a conduit for many different species of epiphytes, insects, spiders, birds, and small mammals in cases of environmental fragmentation, seedsavers' gardens and collections are obstinate spaces carved out from the madness of homogeneity and obliteration. But, one might ask—and the question has been raised—Is this form of conservation intentional, quantifiable, reliable, significant, and replicable? Some may even go as far as challenging if this

is conservation at all. In other words, does it have any meaning or currency in the context of conservation as a scientific and, though less often
admitted, political enterprise?

In a well-cited review entitled "Conservation and Subsistence in
Small-Scale Societies," Eric Smith and Mark Whishnie confronted the
ethnographic evidence on indigenous or small-scale conservationism.
They proposed, "To qualify as conservation, any action or practice must
not only prevent or mitigate resource overharvesting or environmental
damage, it must be *designed* to do so" (2000:493, emphasis added). In
short, according to the authors, two criteria or requirements, namely
effect and design, have to be met; effect alone is not sufficient. Smith and
Whishnie's "theory of conservation" immediately raises a question in
regard to the foregoing discussion: What then do we call the active preservation and transmission of a wide variety of plants by seedsavers, heirloom gardeners, and small-scale farmers? The authors have provided a
handy qualifier (2000:502):

> Our use of "designed" is meant to allow for several distinct pro-
> cesses to play a role in shaping conservation practices. On the one
> hand, it can include design based on conscious beliefs and prefer-
> ences, and hence an intentional form of explanation (Elster 1983).
> But evolutionary processes, whether cultural or genetic, can also
> produce complex design, and our definition also allows this. Thus,
> if it could be shown that a conservation practice had spread or was
> maintained in a population because its practitioners were either less
> likely to suffer extinction or more likely to prosper and spread (as
> compared to non-conservers), that would satisfy the design criterion.

This qualifier seems to me to dilute their main argument, producing a
more functionalist framework, with teleological overtones. While it can
be argued that seedsaving has been favored by evolution because its practitioners tend to persist, if not prosper, I prefer to avoid this conceptual
quagmire and instead to delineate two categories—not requirements—
of conservation, namely *conservation in effect* and *conservation by design*.
These categories sometimes cohere, and other times do not.

Drawing from the works of Michael Alvard (1998), Joseph Soltis et

al. (1995), and Eleanor Ostrom et al. (1999), I define biodiversity conservation as actions or practices that mitigate genetic erosion and involve cost in the short term but secure a collective ecological and cultural good in the long run. For the more formal scientific sector that
employs conservation by design, the cost can be in the form of funding
and training for biological inventories, plant collecting expeditions, gene
bank maintenance, and programmatic or directed in situ conservation.
The cost of protecting biodiversity in the world's agricultural sector alone
runs to approximately $240 billion per year, according to a recent esti-
mate (James et al. 2001). More difficult to pin down, but nonetheless
important, is the opportunity cost of land, energy, time, and other meager resources that are at the disposal of seedsavers and small-scale farmers who willingly forego more lucrative options associated with cash-
cropping or monoculture. The collective benefit is in the form of long-
term maintenance of both biological and cultural diversity, including the
stability, resilience, and other benefits, both direct and potential, that
these ensure for posterity. Note that the strategy or mechanism, whether
by strict design or more idiosyncratic play, is of secondary importance to
the net outcome in this definition.

   I will use institutional programs of on-farm or in situ conservation
as instances of conservation by design and contrast them with seedsaver
conservation of biodiversity as an example of conservation in effect. Let
me stress that these are simply two different forms or kinds of conservation. Both are conscious and, albeit in different ways, deliberate. Moreover, to insist on the design aspect as a prerequisite for conservation is
to exalt all scientific, institutional, and outsider-directed initiatives as
legitimate conservation and to dismiss all informal and local efforts. The
prefixes "para-," "pseudo-," "quasi-," and even, in some respects, "ethno-",
as in parataxonomists and ethnohistory, are all too common and insidious—at one level including, legitimizing, and empowering, while at another level excluding, marginalizing, and patronizing all forms of indigenous or local undertakings. I believe the distinction is an important one
to make in order to illuminate the nature of biodiversity conservation at
the local level and probe any compatibilities or discordances in global
attempts at institutionalization.

Local Resources, Global Science

One way the problem of biodiversity loss has been and continues to be cast is in a straight and narrow economic or utilitarian mode: If we allow biodiversity erosion to proceed unabated, we will quickly run out of landraces and weedy relatives to exploit in order to create our elite culti-vars or our promising cures. Alternatively, it is sometimes framed in a more encompassing biocentric mode: The disappearance of species is now occurring at an alarming rate unprecedented in the history of hu-mankind, or in the considerably longer history of the planet. Either way, the result is to galvanize the scientific and policy community into ac-tion. International and multisectoral organizing and advocacy has suc-ceeded in calling attention to the urgency of the problem and the very real need to do something about it. One watershed document, signed in Rio de Janeiro during the Earth Summit in 1992, is the Convention on Biological Diversity (CBD), which defined biodiversity as "the variabil-ity among living organisms from all sources and the ecological complexes of which they are part; this includes diversity within species, between species, and of ecosystems" (UNEP 1994:4). The CBD thus pronounced as insufficient the conservation of single species in gene banks, or even in protected areas. By the same token, it bound signatory countries to:

> regulate and manage biological resources important for the conser-
> vation of biological diversity, whether within or outside protected
> areas, with a view to insuring their conservation and sustainable use
> (Article 8, c);
> and
> respect, preserve, and maintain knowledge, innovations, and prac-
> tices of indigenous and local communities embodying traditional
> lifestyles relevant to the conservation and sustainable use of biological
> diversity and promote their wider applications (Article 8, j).
> (UNEP 1994:8–9)

Article 8 of the Convention recognized the sovereignty of nations over their plant genetic resources and gave impetus to the conservation of diversity. The explicit recognition of state authority over indigenous community agency in negotiation and decision making regarding conservation and commodification of biological and cultural resources remains problematic, but, for better or worse, the CBD encouraged global initiatives in on-farm or in situ conservation.

Decades of collecting expeditions in what are now called Vavilov centers of crop diversity have led to the preservation of living materials or germplasm outside their normal range, or ex situ, in gene banks, field gene banks, and botanical gardens (for useful reviews, see Plucknett et al. 1987; Cohen et al. 1991; Hodgkin et al. 1995; Maxted et al. 1997). In situ conservation in natural habitats or—in the case of cultivated crops—in farmers' fields, is a logical complement to the conservation of crop germplasm ex situ, but it was mostly dismissed because the overriding concern for production necessitated that farmers devote their land to improved, high-yielding cultivars instead of traditional varieties (Brush 2000). We must realize, however, that this concern was principally driven by state preoccupation to generate surplus from farmers' labor, an agenda operationalized through a concentration on streamlining and efficiency. I suspect another reason is that on-farm conservation was considered too mundane and lacking in "design." This design fetish is also a possible explanation for why in situ conservation in biological reserves and corridors gained credibility and legitimacy long before in situ conservation in farmers' fields did.

In the last three decades, there has been serious reconsideration of this position as even the most well-funded gene banks proved to be subject to human error and prone to degeneration of germplasm viability, on one hand, and cessation or "freezing" of adaptive evolutionary change, on the other (Cohen et al. 1991). Ex situ collections were also found to be more vulnerable to political tensions that affect funding levels, not to mention outright threats to germplasm collections from terrorist attacks (Henry Shands, personal communication, 2002). De-emphasizing these fundamental scientific and political weaknesses, Brush (2000) attributed what he called "shift in attitudes" to the increasing bureaucratic recognition that: (1) in situ and ex situ methods are complementary strategies that address different aspects of genetic diversity; (2) maintenance of genetic diversity does not preclude agricultural development; and (3) conservation of crop genetic diversity by farmers in their fields will not require significant monetary outlays. From a whole complex of motivations, therefore, in situ conservation slowly came into favor, initially with respect to conservation of wild species in protected forest reserves and buffer zones and, eventually, in relation to the conservation of cultivated as well as wild and weedy species in and around farmers' fields. As G. T. Prance (1997:9) pointed out:

> Vital to the future of many crops are the land races of them that are grown by many traditional farmers. Since the tendency has been to replace such traditional systems with modern agriculture, serious genetic erosion is occurring. The best people to preserve these traditional varieties in situ are the farmers and native inhabitants themselves. The in situ conservation of native systems of agriculture could be vital for the future of various crops such as maize and potatoes.

The Food and Agriculture Organization (FAO) and the International Plant Genetic Resources Institute (IPGRI) in Rome are the biggest international players in the increasing prominence of in situ conservation of agricultural biodiversity on a global scale. In an FAO-convened international technical conference in Leipzig in 1996, 150 countries adopted the Global Plan of Action for the Conservation and Sustainable Utilization of Plant Genetic Resources for Food and Agriculture. According to Nuria Urquia of FAO (2001:2):

> The Global Plan of Action provides a coherent, integrated framework for the development of policies for conservation and sustainable use of PGRFA (Plant Genetic Resources for Food and Agriculture), linking ex situ and in situ strategies as complementary to each other. . . . In contrast to ex situ, in situ conservation allows continuous adaptation and evolution of plant populations. In the particular case of on-farm conservation, local cultivated plant germplasm continues to respond to natural and farmer selection pressure, giving rise to a continuous source of adapted improved material. Support to on-farm conservation and improvement of PGRFA can contribute to agricultural development.

For its part, IPGRI has been working since 1995 with national programs in eight countries (Burkina Faso, Ethiopia, Hungary, Mexico,
Morocco, Nepal, Peru, and Vietnam) on a project called "Strengthening
the Scientific Basis of *In Situ* Conservation of Agricultural Biodiversity
On-Farm" (Jarvis et al. 2001). The project seeks to develop a scientific
understanding of farmer decision-making processes that influence in situ
conservation of agrobiodiversity; strengthen national institutions for the
planning and implementation of in situ conservation programs; and expand the participation by farming communities and other groups in its
conservation and use. To date, the IPGRI program has made considerable headway in facilitating the investigation of the biological and social
bases of in situ conservation and has created what they call "a framework of knowledge to support the formulation of on-farm conservation"
(Jarvis and Hodgkin 2000:265). It has made the scientific bases of in
situ conservation more prominent, organized formal community participation, integrated different levels of access and control, and amassed
an impressive amount of baseline data that has not previously been systematically collected in any one project. It has also, however, magnified
a somewhat disturbing discordance, with rigorous science at the center
recruiting, ordering, and valorizing the implicitly undisciplined, unsys-
tematic, and exotic local at the periphery. This discordance needs to be
examined unsparingly and dispassionately in order to evaluate and, if
need be, redirect significant global initiatives.

With a view of comparing conservation by design with conservation in effect, let us examine how the IPGRI project for strengthening
and integrating in situ conservation has been operationalized with respect to: (1) the structure of implementation; (2) the unit of analysis;
and (3) the sharing of information and consensus building. First, I will
describe each of these mechanisms separately, and then I will suggest
some discrepancies between the local foundation of in situ conservation
and the design of national and global programs. Awareness of these discrepancies does not diminish the significance of these efforts; rather, it
can serve as the first step in fine-tuning institutional initiatives so that
they are more in keeping with the spirit of actual, on-site farmers'

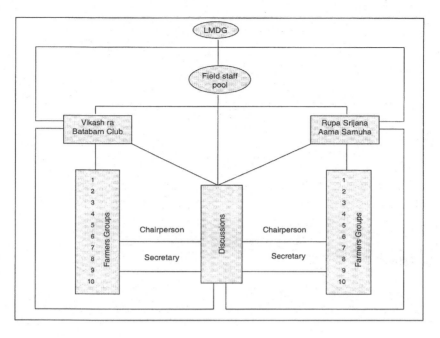

Figure 26 National Framework for Nepal (Source: *A Scientific Basis of In Situ Conservation of Agrobiodiversity On-farm: Nepal's Contribution to the Global Project* [Rome: International Plant Genetic Resources Institute, Working Paper No. 1, 1999])

conservation practices that the global scientific community is trying to emulate and promote.

Two national programs collaborating with IPGRI are Nepal and Hungary, which are represented by "national frameworks" that depict the organization and flow of authority and responsibility (Figs. 26 and 27). Working Paper No. 1 (Upadhyay and Subedi 1999:1–2) describes the institutional framework for the implementation and management of on-farm conservation in Nepal:

> Technical Coordination Committee was consulted as of Memorandum of Understanding (MoU). Botany Division, Executive Director of LI-BIRD and Scientist prepared a list of experts on thematic areas from IPGRI. This was then discussed in TCC. Most of the members of NMDG are from NARC and LI-BIRD. Experts if not available in

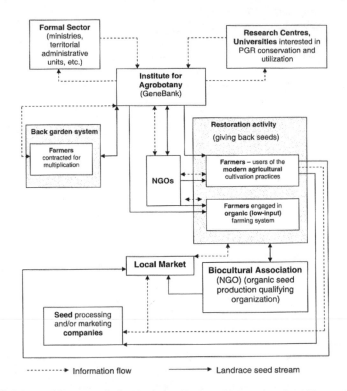

Figure 27 National Framework for Hungary (Source: D. Jarvis, et al., *A Training Guide for In Situ Conservation On-farm* [version I] [Rome: International Plant Genetic Resources Institute, 2000])

NARC and LI-BIRD were invited from DoA and MoA.... Identified thematic experts in the fields of crop biology, social science, participatory plant breeding, gender and community participation were later officially endorsed to work in the project. Three eco-site coordinators are the members of the NMDG by their positions.

The national framework for Hungary is accompanied by this statement (Jarvis et al. 2001):

The existing national PGR [plant genetic resources] conservation structure in Hungary, centered at the Institute for Agrobotany's national gene bank, is implementing on-farm conservation by involving new partners like farmers and NGOs.... Beginning in 1997, new partners were involved to expand the existing programme into on-farm conservation. Regional NGOs are linking with farmers interested in long-term re-introduction and cultivation of landraces with the Institute of Agrobotany, while universities and research centers are investigating the socioeconomic, agroecological and genetic implications of re-introduction. The formal sector [Ministry of Agriculture and Rural Development and Ministry of Environment and Territorial Development] supports this framework.

Jarvis and her coworkers addressed evolving units of analysis in a report to the multisectoral conference on "*In Situ* Conservation of Agrobiodiversity," held at the International Potato Center in Lima, Peru, in August 2001:

> Answers to these questions are being used to develop methods for mainstreaming the use of local crop genetic resources into the agricultural development arena. Key to answering these questions has been the recognition that farmers may characterize the units of crop diversity they manage not by a name but by a set of traits, which the team is now calling "farmers' units of diversity" or "farmers' units of management" or FUDM. This concept, that the "name" may or may not be the level of diversity of farmer management, is now being used to refine methods for using FUDMs in benefit enhancement activities in the farming communities.

In the same report, they also outlined the mechanism of choice for addressing problems of sharing, access, and use of information. The group stated, "Through global thematic meetings, the partners have agreed on common protocols for in situ data structure and management, where each country will manage their own data but have agreed-upon global data variable definitions, data structuring, data cleaning, and data analysis protocols."

Note that in the national frameworks, the arrows, boxes, and levels are predictable in their conformity to structure and hierarchy, suggesting linearity and centralized authority. These are all in keeping with the goal of strengthening the scientific bases of in situ conservation, of course,

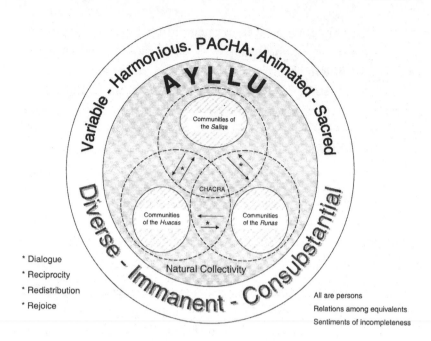

Figure 28 Andean *Ayllu* (Source: T.A. Gonzales, "The Cultures of the Seed in the Peruvian Andes." In *Genes in the Field: On-Farm Conservation of Crop Diversity, IPGRI, IDRC*, ed. S. Brush [Washington, D.C.: Lewis Publishers: 2000])

but one would never guess from the organizational charts that a novel, pathbreaking approach to plant genetic resources conservation, farm-based and farmer-led, is being developed. Contrast the national frameworks with the circular representation of the Andean *ayllu*, which gives a vivid picture of how diversity is cherished and maintained by the local people and how it is viewed as embedded in ever-widening arcs of relationships linking, and thereby strengthening, "incomplete beings" (fig. 28). As described by Tirso Gonzales (2000:203):

> Agrobiodiversity and in situ conservation are foreign terms to the Andean worldview. The local pacha [locality] is central in the Andean cosmology. It encompasses a greater diversity than the term biodiversity. . . . Everything is alive—a mountain, a rock, water,

women, and men—and everything is incomplete. This allows for dialogue and reciprocity in all aspects of existence. All beings are persons in a relationship of equivalents and mutual nurturing [crianza]. At the local level, the chacra [cultivated field] is the place where the dialogue among beings occurs. It forms the basic corner-stone of Andean life. The practice of agri-culture represents the dia-logue which occurs between diverse beings within the natural collec-tivity, the ayllu, the local pacha. The natural collectivity is composed by the communities of the sallqa (nature, where all its members are alive, as opposed to the narrow Western mechanistic worldview), the communities of the huacas (gods) and deities, and the commu-nities of the runas (human beings). At the center of the ayllu we find the chacra(s), and each of them is unique: a major factor under-lying the centrality of locality. The ayllu is found in the local pacha (local landscape) where the three components that comprise the natural collectivity live. The pacha is characterized by being ani-mated, sacred, harmonious, diverse, immanent, and consubstantial. In addition harmony is not given. It has to be constantly procured.

The impression of "business as usual" is compounded by the acronym-izing of farmers' realities, consistent with the fondness for charming and catchy acronyms in the wider arena of international development and conservation. Take, for instance, FUDM for "farmers' units of di-versity management." This concept is probably based on findings that "farmers *manage* rather than conserve on-farm crop diversity. In other words, farmers do not preserve a static portfolio of crops and crop vari-eties on their farms, nor do they prevent introgression from neighbors' fields, field margins, fallow fields, or areas where wild crop relatives grow, but rather they import and discard diversity in a dynamic fashion, ac-cording to their needs in any given period of time" (Cromwell and van Oosterhout 2000:234). However, granting that farmers have a more flexible and dynamic approach to conservation of plant genetic resources does not mean that they do not in fact have an eye toward conserving in the longer term that which they are "managing" in the short term. I would argue further that it qualifies as conservation because that is what it does in effect. We should also not forget that even the most scientific conservation initiative requires incessant—and not always rational—decision making. Given the finite resources of money, time, and energy, not to mention political pressures that change intensity and direction constantly, there is endless adjustment and refining of criteria on what species and varieties deserve a place in "Noah's ark." Since conservation and management invariably go hand in hand, any distinction between the two exclusively with reference to farmers' efforts seems to me rather arbitrary and unjustified. The tendency to conjure another reality through the blessing of an acronym may be quite harmless, but is this new "scientific" coinage really necessary or useful, or is it simply another assertion of inherent legitimacy? I name, therefore I am. What is wrong with "seeds" and "mixtures," "beauty for the eyes," "taste for the palate," and "fragrance for the spirit"?

Equally unsettling is the expressed need to mainstream, systematize, and globalize data-management and consensus-building on what may be quite idiosyncratic but nonetheless effective local practices and habits of mind. The problem I foresee with these mechanisms is that they will then become the indicators of success and thereby define as failure anything that falls short of this elegant and streamlined set of global expectations. Again, one example is the line drawn between "farmer management" and "scientific conservation." This reminds me of what Latour (1993) calls "works of purification" in modern scientific practice. In striving to purge concepts of all traces of murkiness, works of purification are liable to set up false dichotomies, artificial categorical expectations, and standardized forms of compartmentalization that inhibit rather than encourage fruitful cross-fertilization. While international programs on agrobiodiversity conservation are uniquely poised to draw together elements necessary to craft genuine complementation, these initiatives tend to be too *programmatic*, characterized by a continuing attachment to idols of the tribe (the scientific tribe): order, predictability, and uniformity. I have also noticed that, in "strengthening the scientific bases of in situ conservation," there is little tolerance for anecdotes, especially anecdotes of remembrance.

Still, the present climate is much more enlightened than the virtually autocratic appropriation that pervaded plant collecting, conservation, and introduction in the past. In situ conservation is now widely recognized as a necessary complement to ex situ conservation in gene banks. Garrison Wilkes (1991:86–101) calls in situ conservation of economically useful plants "an idea whose time has come." Commodity-focused international agricultural research centers such as the International Potato Center in Lima and the International Rice Research Institute in Los Banos, the Philippines, have joined efforts with FAO and IPGRI in addressing in situ conservation of their mandated crops. In all these efforts, however, one thing that is not adequately acknowledged is that, unlike ex situ conservation, in situ conservation flourished well before scientists ever coined a name for it or elevated it to the realm of "strategy for implementation" or "plan of action." In this, it joins the league of "multiple cropping," "no tillage agriculture," "crop rotation," and "multipurpose trees." Polycultures, from the classical home gardens of Southeast Asia to the *huertas* (subsistence gardens) and zoteas of Latin America to the vernacular gardens of Western Europe and North America, have thrived as in situ conservation sites without much intervention from scientists and policy makers and will likely continue to thrive after "designer" conservation has moved on to yet another trend.

Re-membering Place

The literal translation of in situ conservation is "conservation in place." It may help to keep this in mind in our various attempts to improve upon it. After we have analyzed its different components, it is important to re-member, or put together again, what it is all about in the first place. In essence, local in situ conservation is in vivo conservation, or conservation as a way of life. It is ad hoc, multilayered, nuanced, and complex. We must support, or at least tolerate, the worldviews and lifestyles that undergird diversity if we are to conserve culturally significant plants, particularly if our goal is conservation in farmers' fields.

Two examples of entangled worldviews, actions, and histories that intersect in place can be found in our informants' accounts from Cotacachi,

Figure 29 Garden landscape drawing from Cotacachi, Ecuador, by Maria Gertrudes

Ecuador. Maria Gertrudes, a forty-two-year-old mother of seven, described and illustrated the Andean landscape and the changes she has witnessed while growing up (fig. 29):

> I remember . . . there were native trees like aliso [alder trees], weeping willows, sagalan, cerrotes, cherries, avocados, walnuts, jeriguilla. . . . Then, they began planting eucalyptus, cypress, pine, and eucalyptus has been increasing. In my opinion, eucalyptus should not be planted around the plots because it absorbs all the fertility from the terrains and covers the crops with shade, and dries the land. All the native trees are being lost, all the zanjas [ditches] are no longer like they used to be, and the forest you only see when you go up the mountains. . . .
>
> The crops that we lost are fava beans, quinoa, sweet potatoes,

and, mashua. We don't see these crops very much in the community. The new crops [that have replaced them] are vegetables, blackberries, tomate de arbol (tree tomato), and alfalfa. Before, we did not grow vegetables, blackberries—and alfalfa even less. But our compañeros from the organization gave us the seeds for us to plant. That is how we began planting them and we have continued until today. It is the same with fruits. . . .

With my mother we ate only grains, and we did not have and did not know rice, noodles, and, least of all, sardines. Our diet consisted of corn, beans, quinoa, wheat, barley, and sweet potatoes. Our children do not want to eat grains; they say it hurts their stomachs, too heavy. They find all sorts of excuses to avoid eating [grains] and only want to eat store food such as noodles, pasta, and other treats. . . . When I cook quinoa, they tell me it looks like worms.

From the neighboring community of Morocho, Pedro Lima, a forty-five-year-old farmer and part-time ecotourism lodge operator, described changes from his perspective and expressed nostalgia for the plants his family used to prepare and enjoy:

When I was a child, we used to grow everything that we ate. My favorite food was quinoa and corn soup. We ate chuchuca, barley, wheat, morocho [a kind of corn], colada de morocho con panela [corn gruel with brown sugar], and salty morocho colada [salty corn gruel] . . . To make a favorite salty dish, we used yellow and white carrots, potatoes, and ara papa [wild potato], that we gathered in the mountain. It was small and not bitter and harvested the same time as corn. . . . We used to gather mora [blueberries] and blackberries to sell in the market. . . . We ate wild uvilla [golden berries, like grapes], cultivated and wild tacso, nogal [walnut], capuli [Prunus capuli], and there was another kind of uvilla without covering leaves. Some people have sweet cucumber in the mountain but the lancha [combination rain and sun] ruins it.

In the lower parts, we used to plant everything: wheat, barley, peas, morocho corn, chulpi corn, yellow and white carrot . . . Ocas, mashua, melloco [Andean root crops], and fava beans were planted on the upper slopes of the Cotacachi Mountain. I used to bring down what my grandparents planted. The Morocho community has land on the lake reserve, but today we don't plant there anymore. It has been forbidden by the Ministry. Before we used to plant everything there: wheat, barley, mashua, quinoa, different varieties of potato. These were communal lands. Those people who did not own land planted in communal land, the community would allocate land. . . .

When I was a child, there was no tomate de arbol. Maybe a little bit, but now everyone has . . . I would like to have mashua again, I like it because it is sweet. When one is tired, it is nice to have something sweet. The oca is like that, although when the harvest is coming to an end it must be cooked with salt [no longer put in the sun to sweeten]. . . . Yesterday's food also had less spices. We used lard, salt, onions, cabbage, aliyuyo, and rabano [wild herbs] and berro [watercress] from the stream.

We can see from these oral histories that Andean farmers long for and try to recapture the diversity of plants they grew up with. Connection to place is not measured, or forced, and it has more to do with cosmology and memory than with instructions and flowcharts. Michael Soulé (1993) maps conservation strategies on two critical axes: level of technological and management invasiveness; and degree of social integration. I have situated seedsaver gardens on the lower right quadrant because they are the least invasive of these strategies, with the highest degree of social integration (fig. 30). At the risk of belaboring a point, in situ conservation is *what people do* as they take care of their daily needs and desires, as Andean farmers relate to their intimate-animate landscape in a mutually enriching process of "completion." A comparison of institutional programs of in situ conservation with in situ conservation in the raw, as exemplified by everyday practices of seedsavers and heirloom gardeners, exposes a vexing dilemma: How can in situ conservation, which thrives under conditions of emotional attachment, playful experimentation, and close-to-the-margins coping, be streamlined, systematized, and "made global"? Should it be?

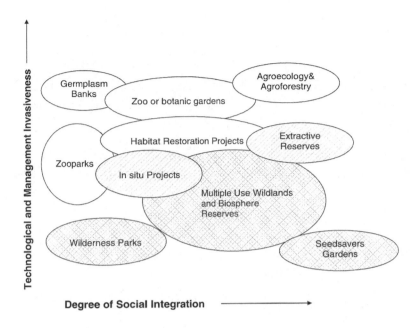

Figure 30 Conservation tactics (Adapted from Michael Soulé, "Conservation: Tactics for a Constant Crisis," In *Perspectives on Biodiversity: Case Studies of Genetic Resource Conservation and Development*, ed. Christopher S. Potter, Joel I. Cohen, and Dianne Janczewski [Washington D.C.: American Association for the Advancement of Science, 1993], 3–17)

Old-Timey Recalcitrance as Counterhegemony

Whereas scholarly (and even, as we have seen, more applied) interest in plant genetic resources and their conservation tends to be weighty and solemn—even pious—local farmers and gardeners have approached the same challenges with a sense of contingency. Describing the penchant for collecting and nurturing adventitious varieties of rice among the Mende of West Africa, for instance, Richards (1996) noted that the names of many traditional varieties are variants of the word "found." One variety is called *tokopoeibun* (in the palm tree), because it was found germinating on the crown of a palm, presumably deposited there by a bird. Likewise, a group of varieties is generically labeled as *helkpo* (elephant dung) for parallel, and obvious, reasons. It goes without saying that adventitious varieties of crops are "found" and become incorporated into the repertoire of culturally recognized varieties only when individual farmers are perceptive and adventurous enough to take advantage of opportunities as they come. It is intriguing, too, that Mende farmers emphasize "finding" over "losing." The process of discovery and incorporation has been referred to by Richards (1996: 226) as "creolization":

> Crop plant genetic resources within the region have been shaped by an ancestral program for the selection and maintenance of a repertoire of duration-specific landraces and niche-adapted genotypes suited for the exploitation of the lowland-upland soil catena under conditions of labor scarcity. This selection template has been applied also to incoming O. *sativa* germplasm, resulting in the spread of more productive and "creolized" farming systems, perhaps based on some exchange between the gene pools of the two cultivated species.

More generally speaking, among seedsavers this corresponds to a certain readiness and alacrity to go after diversity in their collections and their fields, often manifested as an attraction not only to the old and familiar but also to the interesting and the odd. For example, the Hanunoo of Mindoro, the Philippines, set aside a special plot, distinct from their farms, for growing and observing plants that caught their attention along their trails (see chapter 1). In Georgia, Ernest Keheley visits seed stores and browses catalogues just to see and try something different (see chapter 4). In Chanchamayo Valley, Peru, Robert Rhoades encountered a farmer nicknamed by the locals as *El Loco* (the crazy one):

> El Loco was notorious for moving plants or seeds of important crops between extreme climates on the Andean slopes. . . . He uprooted potato seeds from their cool highland home and carried them downhill to the hot, sultry jungle. With banana, he carried it up the mountain to the point he suspected it would not do well just to see what would happen. He was an incurable grafter, planter of many varieties. (Rhoades and Bebbington 1995:296)

It is tempting to identify eccentricity as the key characteristic—or diagnostic feature—of colporteurs. Certainly it is the most visible trait and usually serves as a cue that something interesting is going on. However, eccentricity—or "marching to the beat of a different drummer"—is not the only, nor even the most general, defining quality. More reliable, though perhaps less obvious, indicators include a quiet dignity and personal sovereignty, a significant dose of curiosity and playfulness, sheer tenaciousness, and a sharp native intelligence that is hard to miss. Many colporteurs have gone through conditions of "repression" to different degrees and in various ways. Consequently, they have traveled long and short distances in their lives in search of the "yet-to-become" (Bloch 1988a). In the process, they developed a very strong, and in some cases transportable, sense of place—one that comes across as a willfulness that seems strangely out of place in the marginal spaces they occupy.

According to Michael Dove (1999:61), "The presence of the past in the present—as in the Dayak cultivation of ritual plants—provides, in effect, a transcendence: a mechanism by which the social present—with its narrower, shorter vision—can be transcended." Along the same vein, Bloch insightfully pointed out, "The hero of colportage shows a kind of courage, often like that of its readers, who have nothing to lose . . . the dream of colportage is: never again to be trapped in the routine of daily life" (1988b:183). Seedsavers are purveyors of a very earthy kind of transcendence. In their own way, individual farmers and gardeners who continue to cultivate heirloom varieties and landraces play the role of colporteurs in the conservation of cultural and genetic diversity. Mostly low-status and relatively benign, they do not challenge the existing order (the subtle and enticing totalitarianisms) seriously enough to provoke a backlash but just enough to enliven our memory with discordant notes. The idiosyncratic, "interruptive possibilities" that they pose prevent people from surrendering to the dulling effects of modernity and buying wholesale into the discourse of loss. Through informal experimentation and networking, and a dogged persistence in practices they consider valuable, including the cultivation of plants that are "witnesses of the past," they effectively construct models of alterity that provide reverberating historical contest. Like McClintock's transposable elements, they insert unexpected, faintly subversive, motifs without ever calling too much attention to themselves or their contribution. They never really threaten the central paradigm. But they provide humanity with a pool of options—or, in Gould and Vrba's framework, nonaptations—that may in the end be our only recourse for evolutionary flexibility.

Yet such passions and pursuits are not without cost. I have already mentioned the opportunity cost of deflecting land, time, and energy to nonmarket production of favored species and varieties of plants. There is also the personal strain of pursuing interests at the expense of economic gain (or more basic financial responsibility). One wife of an incorrigible seedsaver who spends virtually all of his waking hours searching for, saving, and sharing seeds all over the southeastern United States revealed to me that she has declared Thursday a "No Seed Day." She intimated that this was for the sake of her emotional balance and sanity. Nonetheless, she and others like her know that seedsavers are working for a collective good. We already know from informal seedsaver networks as well as immigrant gardens, markets, and restaurants that individual nostalgia reverberates through time and space; micro emotions translating into macro challenges to globalization and modernity. Is it possible to measure the pleasure and turbulence, not to mention the integrity and resilience, generated by their actions? Of this I have no doubt, but I will leave this task to someone more creative and mathematically inclined.

Memories Cast in Seeds

In *Memories Cast in Stone*, David Sutton concluded that "history has the potential to be dangerous to the present" (1998:203). But for this to happen, the past, with its "powerful themes and pattern," must be continually engaged in everyday life; it should persist as a "living thing" (1998:203). Seedsavers carry with them their living pasts through the seeds that they collect, grow, and pass along. The pressure of globalization and modernity may suffuse their very existence, but they secure their place through the seeds that they sow and the aroma, tastes, and textures that they harvest and share (fig 31). Whether these farmers and gardeners are rooted in their ancestors' soil or transported to adopted

Figure 31 A Southern seedsaver preparing to cultivate her spring garden (photo by Katie Price)

homelands, their seeds carry intimate personal histories and counter loss of memory and identity. Sutton's analysis is very relevant here: "For part of the very process of globalization is not de-territorialization but re-territorialization: the ways that people in the midst of movement and rapid change are looking for continuity, are looking for 'firm ground under their feet'" (1998:206).

In the previous chapters, I have attempted to tease out the role of marginality and cultural memory in the maintenance of diverse landraces and agricultural practices. As the farmers' and gardeners' life histories amply demonstrate, options and memories are nurtured at the margins, where they are to some degree shielded from development mainstreaming. In the shadow and complexity of the margins, cultural and genetic diversity flourish through mutual protection and reinforcement. As seedsavers' strategies demonstrate, biodiversity conservation does not emanate from, nor is it dependent upon, some exogenous, if well-meaning, "institutional mandate" (Brush 1991). Instead, diversity—both genetic and cultural—tends to be conserved to a greater degree by subsistence cultivators vis-à-vis commercial producers, by women more than men

(Nazarea 1998). Local seedsavers and colporteurs conserve and circulate heirloom seeds as alternative motifs or "dissident opinion" that animate the present, endowing people with a renewed sense of self-determination by allowing a vision not only of alternatives but also of possibilities. Like jumping genes that are activated in times of serious stress to an organism or population, resistance expressed through colportage is activated by mounting frustration brought about by the blandness, predictability, and unmindfulness of modernity. Through heirloom plants, seedsavers make tangible an alternative landscape, a landscape steeped in power and memory.

Bloch's thesis regarding colporteurs, fairy tales, and "wish landscapes" introduced not only choice but rebellion of the kind wherein "the splendor toward which the adventure story heads is not won through a rich marriage and the like as in the magazine story but rather *through an active journey through the Orient of the dream*" (Bloch 1988b:183, emphasis added). To Bloch, raised and rebelling amid the "mush" of middle-class Germany (see chapter 2), the Orient must have signified the outer reaches of the permissible, or even the imaginable. An "active journey through the Orient of the dream," more broadly conceived, is precisely what farmers and gardeners like Braulio de Villa, Francisca Bactol, Matias Benting, Mattie Arnett, Luther Risner, Fanny Lou Bryan, Ernest Keheley, Vi Johnson, Allen Green, Rudolph and Helen Humphrey, Nhan Nguyen Couch, Thanh and Tu Nguyen, and Jose Valverde propel us into undertaking and inspire us into sustaining. While powerful homogenizing forces elide people's pasts, seedsavers and heirloom gardeners nurture sensory stimuli of perceptual recall in the form of traditional varieties of sweet potatoes, black-eye peas, white cucumbers, moon and stars watermelons, and fragrant plumgrannies that sprout in seemingly random abandon, in unlikely places. These discordant notes can make us snap out of forced amnesia and question the inevitability and wisdom of some developments, including (or particularly) those initiated in the name of progress. The significance of individual acts of memory lies in the radiating awakening of the senses that they are capable of stimulating along with the concrete reassurance that one is not alone, or without options.

For, as Elizabeth Tonkin pointed out, "Individuals are also social beings, formed in interaction, reproducing and also altering the societies of which they are members . . . 'the past' is not only a resource to deploy, to support a case or support a social claim, it also enters memory in different ways and helps to structure it. Literate or illiterate, we are our memories" (1992:1).

The requisites of Occam's razor and the imperatives of international research, development, and conservation notwithstanding, local conservation of cultural and genetic diversity in daily life cannot be reduced to a set of governing principles. It is a far more complex phenomenon that requires a much less reductionistic and deterministic framework, as we can see from Julio Valladolid and Frederique Apffel-Marglin's description of the diversity of plants in the Andean chacra:

> The peasants grow diverse and variable cultivated plants in their multiple and diverse chacras. The plants and animals they nurture with dedication and love are members of their families. When the small shoots emerge from the chacra, they are their children; when they flower they are companions with whom they dance and to whom they sing; and when they give fruit at the time of the harvest, they are their mothers. It is, in essence, a ritual agriculture in filigree. It is ritual because one constantly asks permission from the wakas [deities] as a sign of respect, and it is in filigree work because the Andean knowledge of nurturing plants and animals expresses itself in the smallest detail in each specific instance and not in the more general aspects of the cultivating practices. (2001:660)

The more faithful we are to what has for generations existed on the ground, the more effective and relevant our initiatives, mechanisms, and programs will be. Otherwise, we tend toward conservation with strong, faultless design but lacking in metaphor, feeling, or beauty.

Anecdotes, frustrating as they are at times, deserve not only tolerance but also respect from those who seek to understand, reinforce, and employ in situ conservation as an institutional and scientific strategy. They match home gardens in the sense of being somewhat disorganized and full of surprises. To render them otherwise, assuming one could, would be tantamount to stripping them of their meaning and significance. Openness and rigor need not be mutually exclusive, one the province of artists and writers and the other the stock in trade of scientists. McClintock's irrepressible spirit is instructive here. As her biographer, Evelyn Fox Keller, described it:

> In the world of contemporary biological research, McClintock's style is highly idiosyncratic. Her passion is for the individual, for difference. "The important thing is to see one kernel that is different, and to make that understandable," she said. "If something doesn't fit, there's a reason, and you find out what it is." McClintock believes that the prevailing focus on classes and numbers encourages researchers to overlook difference, to call it an exception, an aberration, a contaminant. She sees the consequences as very costly. "Right and left" she says, "they miss what is going on right and left." (1983:xiii)

Purposeful interventions, social movements, and macrostructural changes are important, and so is research that captures these trends. But we run the risk of being little more than "company men" if all we can think of is integrating, institutionalizing, and legitimizing—or worse, claiming that we have somehow invented—something that has been flourishing for ages in individual hands. Just as dispelling ambiguity threatens the power of trickster tales (see chapter 1) and final clarification spells the death of metaphor (see chapter 2), oversimplification and systematization in our representations of, and actions toward, various aspects of biodiversity conservation can doom the spirit that sustains it. Despite their unwieldiness, overlapping and nested circles and webbed networks of relationships need to appear more often than hierarchical boxes and unequivocal arrows in our reports and publications. Tentativeness, partiality, and wonder should be allowed to sneak in more often. There is a story in the Old West about a scruffy old cowboy who rode up to the edge of the Grand Canyon and with great awe contemplated the vast gorge below (Livingstone 2003). He rubbed his chin slowly and thoughtfully and mumbled to himself, "Something happened here."

Like the legendary cowboy, we might more frequently muse, "Something happened here," instead of always (and with great assurance) concluding, "Something needs to be straightened up here." But these remedies only address superficial symptoms, or lapses. I believe what we need is a more fundamental conceptual overhaul: a looser framework, a wider aperture, a less totalizing gaze.

CHAPTER 7

Conservation without Design
Or, The Anthropology of Quirkiness

• • • • • • • • • • • • • • • • • • • •

Moro kohui sullu papa: spotted guinea pig fetus potato
Kkara papa: bitter potato
Yana puma maqui papa: black puma's paw potato
Cuchillo paki papa: the knife-breaker potato
Huira ppasna papa: the fat woman potato
Runtu papa: egg potato
Katari papa: snake potato
Chunta papa: hard wood palm potato
Ttanta papa: bread potato
Aya papa: ancestor potato
Chaucha papa: early potato
Koyu papa: potatoes left in the earth at the time of harvest
Kkehuillu: twisted potato
Unu papa: watery potato
Cachan huacachi papa: potato that makes daughter-in-law cry

—J. G. Hawkes, *On the Origin and Meaning of South American Indian Potato Names*

It is difficult to argue against reductionism and determinacy because they keep science tidy, and, not to be forgotten, because of the undeniable fact that they work. Along the same lines, it is impossible to dislike parsimony because it makes perfect sense that the simplest and the most direct explanation is the best explanation. Imagine if one declared that water seeks its own level *when* the timing is right, *as long as* the ground is smooth and firm, and, yes, *weather-permitting*—and even then, only *certain kinds* of water. Distilled equations, symmetrical tables, and un-equivocal graphs indeed make for elegance, generalizability, and defensi-bility of scientific pronouncements and predictions. They definitely have their place and, at least as far as I am concerned, are much more enlight-ening than endless rumination. Yet, force and cajole as we might, significant aspects of certain phenomena—such as the indigenous sys-tem of naming potatoes, or the local classification of soils on which they are grown—will escape the rigid confines of equations, tables, and graphs. They signify another way of knowing and another logic for organizing, retrieving, and adapting that knowledge (Nazarea 1999).

In the end, the very attributes that make science strong also account for its vulnerabilities and serious limitations. For, in reality, the world that science seeks to explain is not a tidy place, and the most direct explanation, like the consecrated final unified theory, would leave a lot unaccounted for. The world does not owe science an explanation for its cultural and biological diversity. Science itself is a historical, social, and political product. In *Putting Science in Its Place*, geographer David Livingstone argued:

> Like other elements of human culture, science is located. It takes place in highly specific venues; it shapes and is shaped by regional personality, it circles the globe in minds, on paper, as digitized data. For these reasons alone science is as conspicuous a feature of the world's geography as patterns of settlement, the distribution of re-sources, or the configuration of cultural landscapes. . . . Taking seri-ously the geography of science positions the local at the center of scientific ways of knowing. It confirms that the authorized appor-tionment between "the social order," "social context," and "scientific inquiry" is a rhetorical devise that imposes clarity on ambiguity. It renders suspect the idea that there is some unified thing called "sci-ence." That imagined singularity is the product of a historical project to present "science" as floating transcendent and disembodied above the messiness of human affairs. (2003:179)

Highly respected biologists like E. O. Wilson, Paul Ehrlich, Peter Raven, and Michael Soulé have pointed out that the conservation of the world's biodiversity requires not only a rigorous scientific base but also a strong policy response and a drastic cultural reorientation. The formulation and execution of a policy response is difficult enough, but the required cultural reorientation will be painful. This is because, at some point, the big Malthusian scare of resource scarcity, population explosion, and impending famine gained unrelenting momentum, giving rise to technology-worshiping, diversity-dreading monocultures of the mind. This deeply ingrained production and consumption orientation has resulted in a great sense of advancement, abundance, leisure, and pride, and, one can almost say, *untouchability*, at least for the more well-positioned sectors of humanity. Our only recourse now is to search through our "junk" in the "family attic" (Feschotte and Wessler 2001:8923) for uncaptured proclivities, recalcitrant tendencies, and strains of quirkiness that comprise marginalities of the mind. According to Ehrlich, "The cutting edge of the environmental sciences is now moving from the ecological and physical sciences toward the behavioral sciences, which seem to have developed ways to improve that response" (2002:31). But the social and behavioral sciences have issues within the component disciplines, and with the nature of science itself.

Toward a Humbler Science

In anthropology, where the current problem is not so much the link between genes and behavior, or nature and nurture, as that between pattern and change, structure and choice, and system and agency, we have been groping for a stance that would allow a more fluid interpretation of the unity and diversity of human actions in society and environment. At no point has this tension been more keenly felt, or been more sharply divisive, than in the last decade of the twentieth century. When Ortner wrote about practice theory and actor-based models in her article "Theory in Anthropology Since the Sixties" (1984), she could not have predicted the redirection that was on the horizon, one that would not merely fragment but atomize anthropology in the 1990s. The serious questioning of ethnographic authority, timeless representation, and

metatheories based on assumptions of cultural homogeneity and predictability constituted a strong postmodern critique that expressed a dis-
enchantment with science (Marcus and Fischer 1986; Clifford 1988;
Tsing 1993; Steedly 1993; Barth 1993; Abu-Lughod 1993). Critical
thinkers have made the powerful argument that science is about "the
god trick of seeing everything from nowhere" (Haraway 1988:581); that
instead of posing to be neutral, it must make its politics explicit and
define its knowledge production with reference to its ethical position
(Haraway 1989; Trouillot 1991; Fischer 1999).

I believe we need to move toward a science, ironically, *big enough* to
accommodate a less deterministic, less Eurocentric, and less normative
framework. There can be no narrowly prescribed course; indeed, "In
science, as in the rest of life, the paths are paths only in retrospect"
(Weiner 2000:254). The epistemology that deals with facts needs to
acknowledge the hermeneutics that deals in meanings. In many non-
Western cultures, these two spheres of knowing are not necessarily seg-
mented or polarized; they can and do fit in one world. It is interesting to
note that many Nobel laureates come around to this position after as-
cending to the pinnacle of their profession. To everybody's surprise, they
then write books with a strongly metaphysical, moral, and aesthetic bent
and, to the consternation of some of their colleagues (and many science
teachers) around the world, confess that their greatest discoveries arose
more from intuition and serendipity than from adherence to the scientific
method (see, for example, James Watson's *Double Helix: A Personal Account of the Discovery of the Structure of DNA* [1968]; Linus Pauling's
Lifelong Quest for Peace: A Dialogue [1992]; and Ilya Prigogine's *End of
Certainty: Time, Chaos, and the New Laws of Nature* [1997]). Perhaps this
is no accident. While this paradox may suggest that, secure in their ac-
complishments, they can more freely roam and acknowledge fuzziness,
complexity, and flux, it can also mean that they have had this tendency
all along and that this trait was, in fact, what led them to their excep-
tional achievements.

This perspective can loosen up the epistemological and methodological straitjacketing that, in anthropology at least, has been increasingly associated with the scientific, or perhaps more accurately, the scientizing, stance.

In the more applied and interdisciplinary realm, it is about time we stop "monitoring," "harnessing," "impacting," "integrating," "strengthening," and "empowering" local people as if they were "the people without history" (Wolf 1982), or a people without memory. I suggest that we seriously think through Max Weber's introduction to the *Protestant Ethic and the Spirit of Capitalism* (quoted in Mignolo 2000:3–4) so that, fathoming its spell, we may forever rid ourselves of its coercive power:

> A product of modern European civilization, studying any problem of universal history, is bound to ask himself to what combination of circumstances the fact should be attributed that in Western civilization, and in Western civilization alone, cultural phenomena have appeared which (as we like to think) lie in a line of development having universal significance and value.
>
> Only in the West does science exist at a stage of development that we recognize day-to-day as valid. . . . In short, knowledge and observation of great refinement have existed elsewhere, above all in India, China, Babylonia, Egypt. But in Babylonia and elsewhere astronomy lacked—which makes its development all the more astounding—the mathematical foundation which it first received from the Greeks. The Indian geometry had no rational proof . . . the Indian natural science . . . lacked the method of experiment.

Postcolonial and feminist scholars (Anzaldúa 1987; Shiva 1989; Cohn 1996; Mohanty and Alexander 1997; Mignolo 2000; Cole 2001) have questioned this "subalternization" of non-Western knowledge and called for a decolonization of human consciousness and imagination. Such decolonization would require, first, a recognition of a basic epistemic difference that cannot be erased through translation or commensuration; and, second, a foregrounding of other cultures' knowledge bases and an acknowledgment of their situatedness and complexity.

I might add that this effort should not be limited to the erudite problematization and deconstruction of dominant discourses nor confined to the scholarly interrogation of inscription and text. Instead, it should at the same time tackle practices and emotions in all their quotidian detail, mostly of the embodied, sensory kind. Moving away from a monolithic to a hybrid—or, better yet, creolized—epistemology and methodology, we can craft a new scaffolding that would value the contribution of different pathways to the understanding and conservation of biodiversity. Such an approach will allow us to explore inter- and intracultural variation in local environmental knowledge and resource management practices with greater sensitivity and lead to a more in-depth understanding of why, given all the odds, cultural and genetic diversity persist, under what conditions they flourish, and under what pressures they are surrendered or abandoned.

Globalization is bringing these issues to a head by virtue of the increasing "nowhereness" of modern science, markets, technology, and law coupled with the "elsewhereness" of responsibility and morality. In the United States, agribusiness has merged and metamorphosed to such an extent that four giant corporations control the processing of 80 percent of the country's soybeans, 61 percent of its wheat, and either 57 or 74 percent of its corn, depending on the technique (Frank 2004). In India, soybean farmers in rural areas consult a Web-based e-choupal (gathering place) several times daily to keep track of soybean prices on the Chicago stock exchange so they can make better-informed decisions on when to sell and for how much (Waldman 2004). More directly pertinent to this discussion, the Convention on Biological Diversity assigns sovereignty over plant genetic resources to nations, mostly in the South, but provides the instruments and incentives for their secularization and commodification to high-tech or upstream companies, mostly in the North. This has intensified pressures for exploitation through bioprospecting, plant breeding, and biotechnology. At the same time, the emerging policy environment creates layers of authority from the state to the local communities—graduated Little Norths in the South—that subject rightful owners of the plant genetic resources to incomprehensible assessments of ownership and benefit sharing.

A more encompassing framework that acknowledges complexity will allow us, first, to pursue less orthodox, mechanistic lines of research and reasoning; and, second, to foreground agency in the face of officializing metanarratives of the past and the present. If modernity is "forced amnesia," then there is a need to reinforce the range of dreams and choices

that triggers countermemory. In the case of sweeping agricultural modernization that threatens to reify efficiency and uniformity at the expense of stability and diversity, what is called for is the kind of opposi-
tional and subversive countermemory that cultural minorities, women,
and seedsavers elaborate. Countermemory has been variously described
as "subaltern," "counterhegemonic," and "subversive" discourse (Boddy
1989; Stoller 1995), but a more vivid and relevant allusion was provided
by Toni Morrison (cited in Stoller 1995: 31):

> You know, they straightened out the Mississippi River in places, to
> make room for houses and livable acreage. Occasionally, the river
> floods these places. "Floods" is the word they use, but in fact it is
> not flooding, it is remembering. Remembering what it used to be.
> All water has perfect memory and is forever trying to get back where
> it was. . . . It is emotional memory—where the nerves and the skin
> remember how it appeared. And a rush of imagination is our
> "flooding."

Morrison's literary imagery is particularly apt because of the purposeful
straightening that science normally requires and the remembering that
is needed to rescue what has been banished—a remembering or
"flooding" that happens anyway. From this framework, we can more
fully appreciate what, at bottom, marginality and resistance are about,
whether it is ethnic minority resistance to national integration and
women's resistance to gender stereotyping or seedsaver "resistance" to
homogeneity and genetic erosion.

Portraits of Marginality

To weave together the many threads in this book, I explore below what
I consider are some of the best portraits of marginality in the anthropological literature. I will attempt to draw out from these accounts some
crucial aspects of this marginality in order to bring my discussion of
special attributes possessed by seedsavers to some form of conclusion.
Against this backdrop, I will present the story of an informant from

Kabaritan who I came to know very well. For me, she represents *a seedsaver
who could have been,* or, conversely, *a seedsaver deep inside,* that is, someone who possessed all the characteristics of marginality, and all that come
with it, but has somehow, or perhaps more accurately, *was* somehow,
"centralized" and "articulated." It is instructive to examine the process
and consequences of this mainstreaming, on one hand, as well as more
promising prospects of persistence and latency, on the other, in order to
guide external efforts at protecting, or resuscitating, biodiversity today.

Among the most illuminating portraits of marginality in the literature is Anna Lowenhaupt Tsing's reflection on the "marginal queen."
Uma Adang is an unmarried, childless, Meratus Dayak woman dwelling
in the remote rain forest of southeast Kalamantan (Indonesian Borneo),
whose marginality is palpable in about as many dimensions as one can
conceive of. Yet, in her milieu, she poses what Tsing calls (1993:3) "a
disorienting caricature" of motherhood, gender relations, and ethnic minority politics—in short, all power differentials in which she finds herself enmeshed. As Tsing reflects on this out-of-the-way encounter:

> Uma Adang self-consciously offered a perspective from within the
> intersections of a number of dangerous and creative boundary zones:
> the boundary between pagan Dayak and Muslim Banjar, the bound-
> ary between women's role and men's, the boundaries of state rule at
> the edge of the "wild." Reflecting this placement, her perspective
> was syncretic and playful. She was ready to unite old religions or
> create new ones. Even her most playful moods showed deep engage-
> ment with the dilemmas of power and survival on both sides, as well
> as on the boundary. (1993:20)

Tsing provides further insight on Uma Adang's relationship to power:

> I found Uma Adang's eccentric, playful perspectives enormously clari-
> fying. Yet one educated Indonesian, to whom I played a recording of
> one of her speeches, responded, "She's crazy." Even without know-
> ing her local context—in which she is not considered crazy—he
> must have seen how she struck at powerful vulnerabilities in the
> structure of authority, for he added: "She should be arrested." Uma
> Adang's parodic skills helped me see the gaps in regionally dominant

ideologies at the same time that I learned to appreciate Meratus un-
derstandings of the unpredictabilities, absurdities, enormous
power disparities, and creative openings in their regional political
status. (1993:36)

Another evocative portrait of marginality is of a spirit medium and
curer in the Karo highlands of North Sumatra. According to Mary Margaret Steedly, Nande Randal has been a spirit medium since the 1930s.
She learned her craft from the "king of the supernatural wild men," who
taught her about the special herbs that grew on the mountaintop and
about protecting herself from bad spells. She drew her legitimacy from a
Hindu religious book she could not read and was in the peculiar position of being the most senior spirit medium who, partly because of her
gender and partly because of her age, was no longer taken seriously as a
ritual participant by her group. Steedly (1993:8) invoked a Karo expression, "hanging without a rope," to describe Nande Randal's situation
and those who shared her plight in Karoland—those who "felt themselves trapped between the past that was no longer tenable and the present
to which they were, at best, only marginally relevant." Despite this:

> Nande Randal laughed at the photographs I had taken at the *kerja*
> [ritual performed by spirit mediums], justifiably proud of her grace-
> ful appearance and the correctness of form evident even in the still
> pictures of her dancing. In one of these pictures she dances alone,
> stepping high, chin jutting and cigarette clamped in her lips, head
> high and waist wrapped in twined cloths—the plain white cotton of
> the spirits and the red-and-gold embroidered shawls worn ceremo-
> nially by Karo men. As the audience, unseen beyond the edges of
> the photograph, watches attentively, she performs the *tari tongkat*,
> the dance of the magic staff . . . The tari tongkat was once the pre-
> rogative of the male guru, a trained practitioner of the magical arts,
> for whom the tongkat—a long staff carved from the wood of the
> spirit-infested *tenggolan* tree to represent the Karo version of the
> Malay "spectral huntsman" with seven hounds—was a powerful
> supernatural weapon as well as a mark of ritual status. . . . But here in
> a roadside coffee shop . . . Nande Randal moves through the complex

figures of the guru's dance, guided by a spirit perched on her shoulder. Instead of the elaborately carved tongkat, she carries with delicately back-curved fingers, a broom (1993:8)

Next is a story from the belly of the Appalachian coal-mining region of southwestern West Virginia about a woman who transgresses all social codes of proper behavior by "walking on the side of the road." As Kathleen Stewart (1996:61) points out, Eva Mae's actions and her words, delivered with abandon and excess, push underlying tensions and hushed-up injustices to the surface and make "countervailing possibilities tangible by playing them out." Stewart invites us to:

Imagine a world where normalizing discourse is not a norm that people take to but an occasion for restless back talk. Picture Eva Mae. Poor, black, and crazy, she spends her days walking back and forth between [the towns of] Amigo and Rhodell, mumbling to herself and waving a gun or a butcher knife at any car that tries to stop and give her a ride. She acts "the wild mountain woman." Where other women threaten to go crazy, Eva Mae enacts the threat and fashions herself in its image to make herself a walking allegory. Her words are her weapons, and she aims them carefully at the fictions of social order being bandied about in the camps—fictions that delimit "black" and "white" sections of camps and associate men with roads and women with their houses. They say that women walking on the side of the road are either in need of help or looking for sex. Yet women do walk, in pairs and for exercise, and as they walk they dare others to talk. Eva Mae pushes the always already challenged limits of the normal by dressing in a shimmering red dress, huge rhinestone necklace and earrings, and a red wig askew on her head. (1996:60)

Finally, in a fourth portrait, the rupture between rural and urban work—between affirming work for oneself in the countryside and demeaning wage labor for whites in the mines—is crystallized by the creations of the "mad prophet." In presenting the distinctions the Tshidi of South Africa employ and how they act out rather than spell out their preferences and loyalties, John and Jean Comaroff (1987:192) argued that collective consciousness is not to be found in formal institutions but "in the texture of the everyday," not in "explicit statements of common predicament, but in the implicit language of symbolic activity." As the Comaroffs described their revelatory encounter with a madman in a mental hospital:

> His crazy clothes spoke the language of his obsession. His boots, standard issue for mineworkers, were topped by intricately knitted leggings, the painstaking product of many unraveled orange sacks. He wore a cloak and a bishop's mitre, fashioned from black plastic garbage bags. Across his chest was stretched a brilliantly striped sash, on which were stitched three letters: SAR. For his white attendants, these were the most obvious signs of his delusion, although they noted that he also "heard" things. The other patients, however, regarded him as an inspired healer, sent to them in their affliction. SAR was his church, and he its sole embodiment. The letters stood for South African Railways, alongside whose track the hospital lay. In fact, at the very moment we encountered him, the night train for Johannesburg rattled by with its daily cargo of migrants. Later, as we tried to decipher his message, we kept returning, as he did, to SAR. It was a message that spoke directly to his fellow inmates—and to the black paramedical staff. For, in this world of peasant proletarians, the railway forged a tangible link between rural and urban life, hitching together the dissonant worlds of the city and the country. (1987:191)

A few salient features stand out and run through these various portraits of marginality, situated as they are in diverse geographical, conceptual, and methodological locations: the ability to spot and maintain *creative openings* and, while maintaining *correctness of form*, to occasion *restless back talk* that, in the process, conveys a *decipherable message*. Uma Adang, Nande Randal, Eva Mae, and the mad prophet engage their marginalities in uncanny ways that make norms and orthodoxies perpetually permeable and open to challenge. They are peculiar, and spiritual, for not everyone possesses their kind of discernment, or their kind of daring. Seedsavers, though generally less dramatic and more restrained, embody many or all of the same attributes. Their marginality makes them effective and essential agents in the persistence of a countermemory that in turn undergirds conservation of plant genetic resources. Their life histories, their gardens, and their collections make us conscious of alternatives apart from the prescribed and the normalized; *a space on the side of the road* for reflection, transcendence, and transformation. Theirs is *an out-of-the way place*, ripe with possibilities and promise. Their seeds encapsulate memory and constitute a narrative, a tangible link between past and present, between space and place.

An appreciation of these marginalities of the mind is essential in figuring out how best to cultivate and nurture human proclivities that can help us respond creatively and effectively to serious threats for which we have no pre-programmed response. Like jumping genes, they enhance our evolutionary potential and those of other forms of life. However, there is a flip side to this that can be just as instructive: What happens when these capacities are, as it were, "aborted"? What becomes of those who are seedsavers inside but are immersed in overwhelming forces outside? Although postcolonial and feminist studies convince us that modernities are always contested and fragmented, that simple binaries of domination and power are merely intellectual abstractions, and that globalization is invariably permeable and "resistible"—points on which, admittedly, the main arguments of this book hinge—what about the hard reality of local people's own vulnerabilities and the penetrability of the margins? For many of us, caught between resisting and giving in and used to accommodation and compromise at every turn, this situation is extremely easy to empathize with, and it is in this context that I would like to introduce Aling Maring (not her real name). This digression is, I think, necessary to balance any sense of complacency about the unconditional and cost-free persistence of autonomous seedsavers as designated caretakers of biodiversity.

A former landless migrant who arrived in Kabaritan in 1937, Aling Maring was highly regarded as a wife and mother, farmer, and community leader. At the time of my research, she and her husband were amortizing owners of two hectares of irrigated rice field. As land reform beneficiaries, they held a Certificate of Land Transfer to their farmland with a mortgage they were regularly paying off with the Land Bank. Aling Maring came to Kabaritan from the neighboring town as a young girl to help her family because, according to her, her mother was always having babies and her father was having a hard time supporting them. She knew how to plant rice, and at that time, they were planting several traditional varieties like *ginanggang, inaranglan, binato, initiw, Germas, Peta, Binambang, Binicol, Sinantonio, intan, wag-wag,* and *malagkit sungsong.* She also gathered shrimp at night, as her father did, and planted a garden with many different kinds of vegetables by the lakeshore of Laguna de Bay. When the weather was unfavorable for shrimp gathering, she hired herself out as a laundry woman in Los Banos, the university town nearby. She received very basic formal schooling but, during my fieldwork period, she was the secretary-treasurer of the village farmers' organization. Three of her children had finished high school, the other three had completed college degrees. She told me that whereas her husband tends to be protective, she has always encouraged their children to excel and to venture wherever their dreams and desires take them. She credits high-yielding rice varieties and government technicians with their much-improved livelihood. On their farm, all the parcels of irrigated rice field were planted to one variety of rice, IR 42, which they grew for the market. She reserved one parcel for planting a kind of sweet, sticky rice (also an IRRI variety) for home consumption. As she recalled:

> Before—those rice varieties we planted—we just planted them and we didn't have to do anything more; we didn't have to weed, we didn't have to apply fertilizer or insecticide. The rice plants just kept on growing, they did not even get sick; the only trouble they had was being blown over by the wind during a typhoon, the closest they got to being sick was when they were exposed to strong wind and rain and the flowers would be blown off leaving only the panicle sticking out with something that looked like white lard at its tip. And we had time to socialize and take care of the house and look after our children. . . .
>
> Then, the first miracle variety we tried was IR 8, and all of a sudden we harvested 150 cavans [one cavan is approximately equivalent to forty-five kilograms], which was unheard of in those days.

For us, at that time, twenty-five cavans was alright; we spent little but also got little back. . . . We used all the inputs, complete with insecticide, fertilizer, everything that was recommended because if we stuck with the old ways, we would not harvest anything. Technicians were in Kabaritan nearly everyday; early on they even offered prizes like radios for the biggest harvest, this went to the most successful farmer. Pretty soon, though, the people here did not rely on them anymore. We knew what to do. As soon as we saw insects, we sprayed.

Aling Maring's aunt in Kabaritan, the one who raised her, was an extraordinary woman. After the death of her husband, she reverted to her maiden name, an unheard-of practice in the Philippines at that time. She reluctantly acceded to double-cropping of rice when the nonphotosensitive, semidwarf varieties were introduced, but she adamantly refused to try triple-cropping, insisting that "the soil needs to rest, too; you can't keep feeding it and expect it to go without rest." Aling Maring herself was quite spirited and independent minded, her threshold for the preposterous quite low, her sense of humor quick and infective. Yet she gave up on her lakeshore garden and her diverse, traditional rice varieties for the prosperity promised by Green Revolution varieties and technologies.

The example of Aling Maring suggests how science and policy can come together in creative complicity to bring latent tendencies favoring diversity to the fore. A concrete start would be to thoroughly reexamine principles and guidelines for in situ conservation in farmers' fields and to emphasize farmers' knowledge, perspectives, and constraints along the following lines:

1. Recognition of gardeners and small-scale farmers as creators and curators of a significant component of biodiversity, with a wealth of experiences and memories to share;

2. Documentation of local beliefs and practices associated with landraces or folk varieties along with local systems of categorization, evaluation, and management; transmission of this knowledge to the youth

and use of these parameters and insights as the primary bases for setting goals and defining priorities;

3. Conservation of diversity not only in situ but, more fundamentally, in vivo through whole complexes of plant symbolism and usage, including cooking, commensality, healing, ritual, and aesthetics that define identity and sense of place;

4. Evolution of a new language of conservation that does not diminish or patronize farmers' knowledge or ways of life in order to strengthen its scientific base, one that eschews strict requirements of design and celebrates difference, agency, and choice;

5. Acknowledgment of sensory embodiment as being no less legitimate than scientific characterization and prescription; incorporation of cross-experiential learning, including exchange visits, participant observation, and storytelling in finding new ways of communication between farmers and scientists;

6. Extension of support and incentives to seedsavers who propagate and pass along heirloom or old-timey varieties, farmers who practice low-input agriculture and multiple cropping, and women who tend home gardens, for their contribution to conservation;

7. Development of "niche" or specialty markets, along with a new pricing mechanism that would value heirloom crops as well as traditional food and medicinal preparations, and novel uses for old-timey varieties and recipes that would further motivate their producers.

Needless to say, these points have to be thoughtfully debated, refined, and operationalized. In the process new ways of framing questions and addressing problems must be crafted. In particular, the trade-offs between market integration and independence, in other words, between mainstreaming and marginality, need to be carefully teased out and considered not only in light of the short-term but also of the more problematic long-term. In relation to this, it is important to bear in mind that any integration or centering would entail standardization of both quality and measure, and with this, the dark prospect of homogenization. This is already manifest in the present certification procedure for organic produce. It is crucial to develop a robust respect for the significance and complexity of farmers' and gardeners' conservation knowledge and management practices before attempting intervention through any form of market-driven incentive; here I include everything from biodiversity fairs to niche markets. The perspectives of farmers themselves on these matters must be articulated, by them and for them, in this deliberation. In this effort, anthropologists can choose abstraction and detachment, or "ethnographic refusal" (Ortner 1995), but we can also choose ethnographic engagement and draw on our sensitivity and attraction to marginality and "quirkiness," which probably brought us to the discipline in the first place.

From the margins, seedsavers deploy a message of worth rather than protest wherein the currency is joy instead of anger, the motivation hope instead of frustration. Paradoxically, the significance of heirloom gardeners and seedsavers to the conservation of biodiversity is lodged more in what they are not than in what they are. They are not organized, most of them are not inclined to participate in "programs," rarely are they exclusively or even principally motivated by economic considerations, and they are not integrated, linked, or politicized in the obvious sense; in fact, it is likely that they are totally oblivious to their contribution. Yet, in their fields and in their gardens, they contest what is presented to them as "natural" and "inevitable" and in so doing stimulate others to wade through layered memories entwined in food, place, and ritual and other buried sensory experiences from the past. This sometimes confuses us because we like to see their actions as instances of "resistance of the weak." It is tempting to regard them as resistors when they are in fact not particularly interested in proving anything, and to forget that this nonchalance is their greatest source of strength.

Seedsavers pose a subdued but persistent challenge to what those around them take as given and help break the spell of "organized forgetting." Spun in the context of Southern African American marginality, the adventures of Brer Rabbit represents the irreverent, uncaptured spirit in seedsavers and, though somewhat more latent, in all of us. Reviewing the *Tales of Brer Rabbit,* Julius Lester was moved to write:

> While one might want to see Brer Rabbit as Victim, he is not. Neither is he Victor because he is defeated more often than our image of

him might want to admit. The outcome of the Trickster's escapades is not crucial to the tales, nor important even. What is central is the spirit he brings into them. It is this spirit that both attracts us and repels us. We envy it even as we shudder at the thought of emulating it. The essence of Trickster's tales is 'patterned disordering.' This is not the disorder which leads to chaos and destruction. Quite the contrary. It is the disorder that is integral to the ordered pattern of life, that disorder without which life's ordered pattern would become rigid and sterile. . . . Trickster's function is to keep order from taking itself too seriously. . . . Through him, we experience what is not permitted and thereby we are made whole. Not perfect, but whole. (1988: ix)

Although there may be a strong tendency to dismiss seedsavers' individual acts of nonconformity as idiosyncratic (which they are) or mere noise (which they are not), the fact is that they are almost universally present in every agroecological zone and cropping system and their presence and practices "add up." Ubiquitous and irrepressible, they perpetuate disorder by getting away with not planting what is popular, profitable, prosaic, or prescribed. However, it is, as Julius Lester noted with reference to Brer Rabbit, "a patterned kind of chaos," one that forces us not to take ourselves—and modernity—too seriously. It is in this state of play that fairy tales move and alternative landscapes take shape.

Epilogue

• •

Memory thus complicates the rationalist segmentation of chronology into "then" and "now." In memory, the timeline becomes tangled and folds back on itself. Such complication constitutes our lives and defines our experience.
—Richard Terdiman, *Present Past*

Imagine a world sanitized of memories. Picture plants of uniform size, consistent breed, lined up in straight rows, and purged of all companions, allies and enemies both, their function singular and well defined. Envision gardens designed, measured, and controlled; food without ritual, symbolism, and contentment, bereft of all taste, texture, and fragrance. Imagine farmers and gardeners recruited as "the new partners" in in situ conservation, deemed legitimate only after they are trained to follow the rules. Conjure, if you will, a Lamarckian nightmare: kitchens and dining tables shrinking as they become useless, palates and taste buds disintegrating, eyes narrowing as they are permitted to see beauty and power only in lines and levels. Finally, invoke hope that we will never get there.

For this trace of hope, of epiphany and salvation in delicious pleasures that render "all vicissitudes of life unimportant, its disasters harmless, its brevity illusory" (Proust 1934:69), we have to thank seedsavers and their supportive, or at least tolerant, friends and loved ones and the marginal places that sustain them. Individually, theirs is a playful resistance that touches and sustains us all. Collectively, theirs is a force that deters wholesale displacement and abandonment, and loss of memory.

In the words of Proust: "But, when nothing remains of a remote past, after the death of beings, after the destruction of things, only the smell and the flavor, more frail but more lively, more immaterial, more persistent, more faithful, only they last for long."

Here I honor seedsavers we have encountered, along with their very favorites. These plants remain, quaint and quirky but in quiet circulation, because of the curiosity and sovereignty of seedsavers around the world. From the sweet potato memory banking research in Bukidnon, the Philippines, to the Southern Seed Legacy and the Introduced Germplasm from Vietnam Projects in the American South, these incorrigible colporteurs have been and continue to be a never-ending source of inspiration and hope.

Bridge of Seeds and Memory

Conchita and Pio Abadinas: maasin, kalugti, Amerikano, Igorot, kinampay/tapol, 5-finger, klarin

Melencio Avergonzado: banwaanon, tapol, kasindol, katuko, kabuko, banas, Amerikano, klarin, initlog

Ulpiano Amoncio: kamada, Igorot white, Igorot red, kaligatos, binanlao

Lydia vda de Casseres: klarin, taro, 5-fingers/kasindol, valencia, sil-ipon

Matias Benting: binangkal, kalugti, malunsai, kaborong, kuhit-giti/katapok, kabato, tangkalon, karunsing, kabato/senorita, kamada, lila, 5-finger, initlong, seventy-days

Teodoro Binanlao: Zamboanga, klarin, turay, malanaw, lamputi, makalugsok, kulating, Valencia, buwan-buwan, sinundalo, 5-finger, linggatos, laguitlit, lutia

Felomeno and Gloria Dobleano: klarin, lambayong

Marcosa Fuentes: kasindol, kinampay, kabutho, initlog

Concordia Gerong: kasindol, Amerikano, kabutho, bilaka, klarin, katuka, kalugti, manabang

Aurilla Maglupay: lutia, Valencia, Amerikano, kalugti, kabus-ok, 5-finger, kinampay, sil-ipon, initlog

Conchita Recisio: Amerikano, klarin, 5-finger, Igorot, tapol/kinampay

Rosita Tamayo: klarin, Valencia, 5-finger, kamada, Igorot, Imelda, kabato
Magna Asilan: binawil, Valencia, kauyang, lambayong, lamputi
Francisca Bactol: si-uron, lambayong, kamba, kalibre
Dominga Balaon: initlog, manugyang, lamputi, kalibre, Malaybalay, subat, lawaton
Erlinda Cajiles: klarin, kasindol, kamada, kalibre
Emeliano Cuno: kauyag, si-uron, kulating, lambayong, kamba, sugahak, kinampay, manugyang, atay-atay, tinangkong
Felix Data: Malaybalay, kamba, Imelda, si-uron
Elena Gayunan: initlog, si-uron, linggatos, klarin, meguga, kabus-ok, turay
Amecito Humunlay: kalugti, lambayong
Betty Mamatan: lambayong, si-uron, Amerikano
Villamin Mal-eng: lambayong, Valencia, si-uron, initlog
Karen Askren: Aunt Zora dry bush beans
Jimmie Atkins: yellow corn
John Blackmon: nest onions
Oliver Clark: red and yellow squash; red and orange habanero, Irish bonnet, Charleston hot, Peter, and cowhorn hot peppers
George Eason: mole beans, castor beans
J. S. Fair: pole white butterpeas
B. J. Holion: pole red speckled butterpeas, jubilee watermelon, tender sweet yellow watermelon
H. O. Holley: moon and stars watermelon, cowhorn hot pepper
K. H. Ingle: blue collards, Grandma's black beans, 2 pear tomato varieties, cowhorn okra
Jeanne McKay: Israeli melon, Ogen melon
Clayton G. Metcalf: Peter pepper, Sally Hades's white eggplant, Jerusalem cherry, dipper gourds
Joyce Neighbors: approximately 200 old southern apple varieties
Sam J. Reid: white whippoorwill, black crowder, hog brains, old-timey black cornfield, old-timey stick blue beans
Sheila Smith: celosia, red salvia, lemon drop marigold, red cypress vine, pumpkins
Katherine Adam: purple pod pea, Beste von Allen wax bean
Don Robinson: old-timey pumpkin seeds, watermelon-shaped pumpkin

Robin Kirk: Jamaican amaranth, papayas, key limes, heat-tolerant tomatoes and corn

B. McClellan: old-fashioned small white cucumber

Katherine Mills: turnips, heat-resistant tomatoes, sweet peppers, dent
corn

A. Pease: bottleneck gourds, banana gourds, triangle gourds, pumpkin
gourds, martin gourds, wren gourds, penguin gourds, bushel gourds,
canteen gourds, luffa gourds

Vaughan Allison: broom corn seed

Claudine Arnsdorff: collards, purple hulled peas, red hulled peas

Shelby Baker: Toole cotton, Cook cotton

Talmadge Beasley: seed cane

A. Bennett: southern field peas

H. Bent: black-eyed Susan

S. W. Boatright: yellow moon and stars watermelon

William Bonner and Family: old-fashioned green sugarcane

Richard Bradford: tomatoes—jumbo Genoa, pink beefsteak, sundrops,
tigerella, prudens purple, santiam, bulgeiss climbing triple crop, fakel,
evergreen, fireball, Principe Borghese, Wilamette, Arkansas traveler,
green zebra, big rainbow, sausage, jubilee, ruffled, brandywine, pink
grapefruit, baby pink oxheart, russo sicilian togetta

Aubry Brady: touch-me-nots, four o'clocks, everbearing strawberry

Judy Brewer: blueberries

H. M. Burnette: moon and stars watermelon, old-timey plumgranny

Fannie Lou Bryan: old-fashioned white crispy cucumber

Charles Burnette: plumgranny

Bob Burns: African winter squash, Florida lettuce

Roy Caine: white peach

M. W. Callaway Sr.: pure willow, butter bean

Jan Cash: gourd, herbs

Greg Caudel: Texas longhorn okra

Jeff Champion: old-timey plumgranny

Gwyn Chestnut: sunburst tomato

Margie Clark: old-fashioned canna lilies

James Coleman: old-fashioned red poppy Daug seed

Wayne Collins: plumgranny

Ollie Conley: althea

Christopher Herty: sugar baby watermelon, black krim tomatoes, horse-
     radish, comfrey, various flowers

L. Day: red sugarcane

A. Dee DeVille: ping-tung eggplant, pre-1865 cowhorn okra, lamb quar-
     ters, black tail mountain watermelon

Guy Dodd: old-fashioned shallots

B. Dykes: giant pumpkin

Lois Foerster: country gentleman corn, okra, mammoth melting peas,
     plumgranny

Harold Fowler: old-fashioned multiplying onions

John Gardner: winter squash, bloody butcher corn

Dolly Gray: real good watermelon

Mark Harp: old-fashioned sweet corn

Ed Harris: sorghum

Carol Hayes: gourds

H. Hemphill: old-fashioned pink amaryllis

Betty Hickox: old-fashioned gladiolas

Leonard Hill: hot old-timey cowhorn pepper

Thelma Hines: old-timey plumgranny

Ivan Holbrook: old-timey yellow watermelon

Marion Hunt: plumgranny

Chris Inhulsen: calico pea, Mexican top pumpkin, big frosty pole bean,
     pink-eye butterbean, cushaw melon, Braoddus bean, Whatley's
     prolific, Holstein cowpeas, Lynch butterbean

L. V. Itson: hot peppers, yellow squash

Naomi Isaacs: old-timey tomato

G. Ison: thornless blackberry

Mike Jinglewski: rooster spur hot pepper

Vi Johnson: purple hulled pea, black-eye pea

Connie Jones: old-timey roses

Retha Jones: multiplying onions

Dorl King: old-timey white self-pollinated corn

Gerard Krewek: Seminole and cheese pumpkins

Ernest Keheley: white crowder pea, Hastings cornfield bean, big boy pea,
    martin gourd, whippoorwill pea, crowder pea, Hickory King, Hastings
    corn mixed bean, Hercules pea, red ripper pea, west 6-week's pea,
    pink-eye pea, colossus, pink-eye purple hull, cantaloupe, Hastings
    white corn, blue goose bean, knuckle hull crowder pea, purple hull
    pea
Jim Lawson: old-timey varieties of limbertwig apples, super dwarf apple
Shirley Ledbetter: old-timey colored butterbeans
Melvin Lewis: running okra, pomegranate
B. Lunsford: old-timey daffodil bulbs
Pat Lystiuk: old-fashioned phlox
Joe Mason: peas, beans, corn, okra, watermelon
Ed McDade: longneck dipper gourd seeds
J. McMahon: orange flowered gladiolus
R. C. Morgan: pole red ripper cowpeas
Blake Ortman: African squash, red sweet potato, white sweet potato
Harriet Parnell: bird's eye hot peppers
Floyde Payne: old-timey plumgranny
Houston Phillips: old-fashioned green cane
Emmett Pipker: butterbeans
M. L. Powell: rooster spur hot pepper
Freida Rahn: moon and stars watermelon
Dell Ratcliffe: multiple corn, unknown butterbean, red okra, Chinese
    lantern
Patricia Reynolds: yellow crookneck squash
Herbert Rice: Jerusalem artichokes
Clark Robinson: black pole string beans, black-eye peas
Richard Rowe: moon and stars watermelon
L.M. Sasser: moon and stars watermelon
Betty Savage: marigold
G. Savage: caveman's gourd
George Sigmon: old-timey cantaloupe
Phil Sims: white velvet okra
E. Smith: red delicious watermelon
Hubert Sowell: yellow moon and stars watermelon

R. E. Stallings: running okra, calico cowpea, late running pea, late running cowpea, brown turkey, blue goose combine, clay peas, colossus cowpea, big boy, Mississippi purple hull

Beatrice Teague: plumgranny

Willie Thomas: yard-long beans, field peas, collards, seven top turnips, purple top turnips

N. H. Wallace: old-timey sweet yellow collard

LaVon Wood: June-bearing strawberry plants

Mossie N. Gross: speckle fall bean, Washington-fall bean, Hasting bean white pole

Mattie Arnett: white bunch bean, greasy grit/forty bushel bean, sweet salad peas, plumgranny

Harold Martin: blackheart cherry

Rodney Owens: rhubarb

Dorothy Porter: sunflower, yellow squash

Walter Reichert: Georgia rattlesnake watermelon, New Mexico cave bean, Jacob's cattle bean, sacrament bean, big pumpkin, large speckled Christmas lima, Angie's WPA bean, Kansas black pole lima, black crowder, Cherokee trail of tears pole green bean, Missouri yellow-flesh watermelon, Lynch's collection pole lima

Frank Adkins: silver-tip cowpea, Aunt Bea's half runner snap

Claude Bowman: Red Indian, cling, and freestone peaches

Lee Calhoun: whippoorwill pea, smitty pea, red ripper pea, Calcutta peas, Ledmon watermelon, *Citrullus lanatus*, percules crowder pea, black cowpea

Barry Cox: cockscomb

Margaret Lail: climbing okra, mole beans, Peter pepper, tree pepper, butternut squash, cucumber

Maurice Marshall: over 400 heirloom apple varieties

E. R. Mercimore: moon and stars watermelon, white cucumber, old-timey pie pumpkin, sugar pumpkin, mellar squash, cowpeas

Chuck and Peggy Patrick: butter peas, greasy cutshorts, winter onions, elephant garlic, wild ginseng, golden seal, Indian corn, candy roaster pumpkins, winter squash, 5 kinds of mint, Jerusalem artichokes, horseradish

A. C. Sossomon: pomegranate

D. C. Southards: paw paw, old hybrid cannonball

Ida Thomas: black crowder pea, Myrtle Garmon pea

Janet Wilson: bunch beans, bush beans

Alice Yeaman: trail of tears bean, pole October bean, Logan Glaret bean, Hidatsa shield figure bean, black soup bean, bird egg bean, old-fashioned pumpkin, Mama Share's tomato, Auna Russian tomato, Cherokee purple tomato, Alice's favorite pepper, yellow hot pepper, Ecuadorian legitt green pepper, Peruvian long pepper, top set garlic, cayenne garlic, creole garlic

Laura Young: speckled pole butterbeans

Carl and Karen Barnes: red ripper pea, black crowder pea, several Native American corn varieties, white cushaw squash

James Nicholson: Florida Seminole pumpkin

Eddie and Janet Gordon: Thai pepper, horseradish

Clark Beavans: brandywine tomato, moon and stars watermelon, habanero chili pepper

Ruby Browning: 6-week pea, antique crowder, antique pale string bean, pale antique green bean, moon and stars watermelon

Jimmy M. Cooley: ham and gravy peas

Charles E. Martin: black crowder, red ripper cowpea, black peanuts, white peanuts, Petosky cantaloupe, Cuba black watermelon, cowhorn okra, pencil cob corn, Holcombe prolific corn, white sweet potatoes, creamy black beans, martin gourds, Peter peppers

Dot McHargue: castor beans, martin and bushel gourds, garlic chives, Peter peppers

Gary Adcock: egg gourd

Patricia Brady: old-timey whippoorwill cowpea

Oda Cherry: corn, cabbage, butterbeans, plumgranny, half runners, stake beans

Mary Cole: pinto beans

John Coykendall: butterbean—snow-on-the-mountain butterbeans, purple eye pole butterbeans, shanty boat butterbeans, king of the garden butterbeans, Civil War butterbeans, old-timey golden stick pole beans, granny bean, tick bean, white hull pink tip, milk and cider pole beans, turkey craw bean, preacher peas, washday peas; corn—yellow shoepeg, white shoepeg, Hickory King; and many more

Lisa Bender: over 150 varieties of herbs and wildflowers, deer tongue lettuce, Cherokee pole bean

Terry Doss: plumgranny, cushaw

Clatie Dyer: rice pea, red ripper pea, moon and stars watermelon

B. Sue Eldridge: red beans, cypress vine, passion vine

Matthew English: hyacinth bean, cucuzzi, purple lambs quarters

Sheryle: pomegranates

Betty Jo Hancock: sisters rose

Mitchell T. Hardin: German queen and Japanese pink heirloom tomatoes

LeAnne Hawn: four o'clocks

Donna Hudson: turkey craw bean, big Washington bean, succotash beans, steel blue cross, cutshort bean, white creaseback bean, wild turkey pea, wrinkle seeded purple hull pea, Robbins melon, wild goose pea, rattlesnake pea, Mary Seo's blackbean, Franklin County bean

Rudolph and Helen Humphrey: Kentucky field pumpkin, cutshort bean, wild turkey bean

Brenda Lessman: tobacco field bean, white crowders

Ruth Longmire: stick bean, white cornfield bean, stooksbury bean, Longmire bean, brown bunch bean, yellow bunch bean

Jeff Poppen: Mrs. Biler butterbean, Bradly tomatoes, hardy kale

Carroll Raines: moon and stars watermelon, habanero peppers

Lisa Robinson: cherry tomatoes, birdhouse gourd, luffa, pink hollyhocks, white columbine, whirligig zinnia, sunflowers

Ethel Loy: greasy black bean, shelley bean, white half runner, Longmire bean, brown bunch bean, turkey bean, 1000–1 bean, Rutger's tomato, Alabama Jubilee sweet potato, white queen sweet potato, Hickory King corn

Sunday Rogers: Queen Anne's lace, goldenrod, gay feather, pokeweed

Chris Sewell: snow-on-the-mountain butterbean, red butterbean

R. Stanley Slatton: Reid's yellow dent corn, looney white corn, case knife beans

Melvin Mustard: Johnson bean, cutshort bean, black pod bean, greasy
   back bean, red okra
Clive and Shelly Valentine: sorghum
Joy Bannan: brandywine, Cherokee purple and red currant tomatoes
Peggy L. Cornett: tennis ball lettuce, McMahon Texas bird pepper, cy-
   press vine, Prince Albert pea
Ryan McNeil: Carolina black peanut, Carolina gold rice
Linda Yates: sweet pickling pepper
Nhan Thanh Couch: khô qua (bitter melon), bâu (bottle gourd), muop
   (loofah), he (chives)
Dang Nguyen: ngò ri (coriander)
Thanh Nguyen: móng tay (garden balsam), khô qua (bitter melon)
Nghia Tran: ot hiêm (hot pepper)
Thanh Quach: Angel's hair
Bao Pham: sa-bô-chê (sapodilla), la ban (tree)
Mung Fowler: dau đen (black bean)
Roselyn Le Do: rau đai (type of mint), hôt cai be xanh (type of mustard),
   me ngot (sweet tamarind), star fruit, mông toi (malabar spinach),
   khô qua (bitter melon), sugar apple, grapefruit, cang cua (peperomia),
   hue (Thai basil), ńgo gai (long coriander), papaya
Trung Van Nam: rau đai (Vietnamese mint)
Gon Nguyen: rau tan (Vietnamese mint), hung cay (spearmint), truc
   (bamboo), rau ram (Vietnamese coriander), rau ma (pennywort),
   rau lan (sweet potato), hue (Thai basil), ca (tomato), dau bap (okra),
   ca tim (eggplant), bau (bottle gourd), dua leo (cucumber), ot (pepper), rau muong (water spinach), rau ngo om (rice paddy herb), rao
   dang (Vietnamese herb), he (chives), rau thom (Vietnamese herb)
Jimmy Tran: tia to (beefsteak plant), sa (lemongrass), bac ha (type of
   taro), rau ram (Vietnamese coriander), cay cam (orange tree), kinh
   gioi (marjoram), nhap ca (Vietnamese mint)

Notes

• •

Chapter 1

1. In Green Revolution parlance, "well-endowed areas" are those that are flat, irrigated, close to the market, and with capital for technology adoption; in other words, areas wherein the introduction of new varieties and technological packages is likely to succeed.

2. Elite varieties or lines have been highly manipulated by plant breeders and thus considered as products of advanced selection, in contrast to farmers' varieties or landraces that are sometimes considered as primitive, raw materials for plant breeding and bio-technology.

3. Ecotones are transitional zones between two different types of environments or communities that are each characterized by richer resources and diversity than ei-ther of the two communities (Odum 1971; Rhoades 1974; Withers and Meentmeyer 1999). Borders or borderlands parallel ecotones in the sense that they are junctures between two nations or cultures where contrasting ideologies proliferate and conflicts and tensions are resolved through ambiguities and multiple identities (Anzaldúa 1987; Alvarez 1995; Saldivar 1997).

4. By "inevitable," I am referring to the narrowing of alternatives for local farmers until the only remaining course of action is the adoption, and increasing reliance on, commercial agriculture.

References

• •

Abercrombie, Thomas Alan. 1998. *Pathways of Memory and Power: Ethnography and History Among an Andean People.* Madison: University of Wisconsin Press.

Abu-Lughod, Lila. 1986. *Veiled Sentiments: Honor and Poetry in a Bedouin Society.* Berkeley, Calif.: University of California Press.

————. 1993. *Writing Women's Worlds: Bedouin Stories.* Berkeley, Calif.: University of California Press.

Airriess, Christopher, and David Clawson. 1994. Vietnamese Market Gardens in New Orleans. *Geographical Review* 84(1):16–31.

Akimoto, Masahiro, Yoshiya Shimamoto, and Hiroko Morishima. 1999. The extinction of genetic resources of Asian wild rice, *Oryza rufipogon* Griff.: A case study in Thailand. *Genetic Resources and Crop Evaluation* 46 (4): 419–25.

Alcorn, Janis B., and Margery L. Oldfield, eds. 1991. *Biodiversity: Culture, Conservation, and Ecodevelopment.* Boulder, Colo.: Westview Press.

Altieri, Miguel A. 1999. The ecological role of biodiversity in agroecosystems. *Agriculture, Ecosystems, and Environment* 74: 19–31.

Alvard, Michael S. 1998. Evolutionary ecology and resource conservation. *Evolutionary Anthropology* 7: 62–74.

Alvarez, Robert R., Jr. 1995. The Mexican–U.S. border: The making of an anthropology of borderlands. *Annual Review of Anthropology* 24: 447–70.

Anzaldúa, Gloria. 1987. *Borderland/La Frontera: The New Mestiza.* San Francisco: Aunt Lute Books.

Appadurai, Arjun. 1991. Global ethnoscapes. Notes and queries from a transnational anthropology. In *Recapturing Anthropology: Working in the Present*, ed. E. G. Fox. Santa Fe: School of American Research.

Arthur, W. Brian. 1999. Complexity and the economy. *Science* 284: 107–9.

Babcock, Barbara. 1985. A tolerated margin of mess: The trickster and his tales reconsidered. In *Critical Essays on Native American Literature*, ed. A. Wiget, 153–85. Boston: G. K. Hall.

Ballinger, Franchot. 1989. Living sideways: Social themes and social relationships in Native American trickster tales. *American Indian Quarterly* 13: 15–30.

Barnes, Carl, and Ellen Gray. 2004. *Survey of Seedsaving Networks and Resources.* Saving Our Seed Project (Unpublished).

Barth, Fredrik. 1993. *Balinese Worlds.* Chicago: University of Chicago Press.

Basso, Keith. 1996. Wisdom sits in places: Notes on a Western Apache Landscape. In *Senses of Place*, ed. S. Feld and K. H. Basso, 53–90. Santa Fe: School of Americas Research.

Beattie, Andrew, and Paul R. Ehrlich. 2001. *Wild Solutions: How Biodiversity is Money in the Bank.* New Haven, Conn.: Yale University Press.

Berry, Wendell. 1990. *What are People For?* New York: North Point Press.

Blaeser, Kimberly M. 1995. Trickster: A compendium. In *Buried Roots and Indestructible Seeds*, ed. M. Lindquist and M. Zanger, 47–66. London: University of Wisconsin Press.

Bloch, Ernst. 1988a (1930). The fairy tale moves on its own in time. In *The Utopian Function of Art and Literature: Selected Essays*, ed. J. Zipes, 163–66. Cambridge, Mass.: MIT Press.

———. 1988b (1958). Better castles in the sky at the country fair and circus, in fairy tales and colportage. In *The Utopian Function of Art and Literature: Selected Essays*, ed. J. Zipes, 167–85. Cambridge, Mass.: MIT Press.

———. 1991. *Heritage of Our Times.* Trans. Neville and Stephen Plaice. Berkeley, Calif.: University of California Press.

Boddy, Janice. 1989. *Wombs and Alien Spirits: Women, Men, and the Zar Cult in Northen Sudan.* Madison, Wis.: University of Wisconsin Press.

Braudel, Fernand. 1980. *On History.* Trans. Sarah Matthews. Chicago: University of Chicago Press.

Brewer, Ebenezer Cobham. 1898. *Dictionary of Phrase and Fable.* Philadelphia: Henry Altemus Company.

Brush, Stephen. 1991. A Farmer-based approach to conserving crop germplasm. *Economic Botany* 45: 153–65.

———. 1992. Reconsidering the Green Revolution: Diversity and stability in cradle areas of crop domestication. *Human Ecology* 20: 145–67.

———. 2000. The issues of in situ conservation of crop genetic resources. In *Genes in the Field: On-Farm Conservation of Crop Diversity*, ed. Stephen B. Brush, 3–26. Rome: International Development Research Centre and International Plant Genetic Resources Institute.

Bureau, Thomas E., and Susan R. Wessler. 1994. Mobile inverted-repeat elements of the Tourist family are associated with the genes of many of the cereal grasses. *Proceedings of the National Academy of Science USA* 91: 1411–15.

Byrne, David. 1998. *Complexity Theory and the Social Sciences: An Introduction.* New York: Routledge.

Calhoun, Creighton Lee. 1995. *Old Southern Apples*. Blacksburg, Va.: McDonald and Woodward Publishing Company.

Camacho, Juana 2001. *Mujeres, zoteas y hormigas arrieras: Prácticas de manejo de flora en la costa Pacífica chocoana*. In *Zoteas: Biodiversidad y Relaciones Culturales en el Chocó Biogeográfico Colombiano*. Medellin, Colombia: Instituto de Investigaciones Ambientales del Pacifico, Fundacion Natura, Fundación Swissaid, and Intempo.

Campbell, Donald Thomas. 1965. Variation and selective retention in sociocultural evolution. In *Social Change in Developing Areas*, ed. H. R. Baringer et al. Cambridge, Mass.: Shenkman Publishing Co.

Chapin, F. Stuart, Osvaldo E. Sala, Ingrid C. Burke, J. Phillip Grime, David U. Hooper, William K. Lauenroth, Amanda Lombard, Harold A. Mooney, Arvin R. Mosier, Shahid Naeem, Stephen W. Pacala, Jacques Roy, William L. Steffen, and David Tilman. 2000. Consequences of changing biodiversity. *Nature* 405: 234–42.

Claude the Colporteur. 1854. *Putnam's Monthly Magazine of American Literature, Science and Art* 4: 227.

Clifford, James. 1988. *The Predicament of Culture: Twentieth-Century Ethnography, Literature and Art*. Cambridge, Mass., and London: Harvard University Press.

Cohen, Joel I., J. Trevor Williams, Donald L. Plucknett, and Henry Shands. 1991. *Ex situ* conservation of plant genetic resources: Global development and environmental concerns. *Science* 253: 866–72.

Cohn, Bernard S. 1996. *Colonialism and its Forms of Knowledge: The British in India*. Princeton: Princeton University Press.

Cole, Jennifer. 1998. The work of memory in Madagascar. *American Ethnologist* 25: 610–33.

———. 2001. *Forget Colonialism? Sacrifice and the Art of Memory in Madagascar*. Berkeley: University of California Press.

Comaroff, John, and Jean Comaroff. 1987. The madman and the migrant: Work and labor in the historical consciousness of a South African people. *American Ethnologist* 14: 191–209.

———. 1993. *Modernity and its Malcontents*. Chicago: University of Chicago Press.

———. 1997. *Of Revelations and Revolutions: The Dialectics of Modernity in a South African Frontier*. Chicago and London: The University of Chicago Press.

Comfort, Nathanial C. 2001. *The Tangled Field: Barbara McClintock's Search for Patterns of Genetic Control*. Cambridge, Mass., and London: Harvard University Press.

Conklin, Harold. 1957. *Hanunoo agriculture in the Philippines*. FAO Forestry Development Paper 12. Rome: Food and Agriculture Organization.

Connerton, Paul. 1989. *How Societies Remember*. Cambridge: Cambridge University Press.

Cragin, Thomas J. 2001. The failings of popular news censorship in nineteenth-century France. *Book History* 4: 49–80.

Cromwell, Elizabeth, and Saskia van Oosterhout. 2000. On-farm conservation of crop diversity: Policy and institutional lessons from Zimbabwe. In *Genes in the Field: On-Farm Conservation of Crop Diversity*, ed. Stephen B. Brush, 217–38. Rome: International Development Research Centre and International Plant Genetic Resources Institute.

Daily, G. C., ed. 1997. *Nature's Services: Societal Dependence on Natural Ecosystems*. Washington, D.C.: Island Press.

DeMuth, Suzanne. 1998. *Vegetables and Fruits: A Guide to Heirloom Varieties and Community-based Stewardship*. Beltsville, Md.: United States Department of Agriculture.

Donald, C.M. 1968. The breeding of crop ideotypes. *Euphytica* 17: 385–403.

Dove, Michael. 1999. The agronomy of memory and the memory of agronomy: Ritual conservation of archaic cultigens in contemporary farming. In *Ethnoecology: Situated Knowledge/Located Lives*, ed. Virginia D. Nazarea, 45–69. Tucson: University of Arizona Press.

Edelman, Marc. 2001. Social Movements: Changing paradigms and forms of politics. *Annual Review of Anthropology* 30: 285–317.

Ehrlich, Paul R. 1988. The loss of diversity: Causes and consequences. In *Biodiveristy*, ed. E. O. Wilson, 21–27. Washington, D.C.: National Academy Press.

————. 2000. *Human Natures: Genes, Culture, and the Human Prospect*. Washington, D.C.: Island Press.

————. 2002. Human natures, nature conservation, and environmental ethics. *BioScience* 52: 31–43.

Elster, Jon. 1983. *Explaining Technical Change: A Case Study in the Philosophy of Science*. Cambridge, U.K.: Cambridge University Press.

Escobar, Arturo. 1995. *Encountering Development: The Making and Unmaking of the Third World*. Princeton: Princeton University Press.

————. 1998. Whose knowledge? Whose nature? Biodiversity, conservation, and the political ecology of social movements. *Journal of Political Ecology* 5: 54–82.

Espeland, W. N., and M. L. Stevens. 1998. Commensuration as a social process. *Annual Review of Sociology* 24: 313–43.

Fedoroff, Nina V. 1984. Transposable genetic elements in maize. *Scientific American* 250: 84–99.

Ferguson, James. 1990. Mobile workers, modernist narratives: A critique of the historiography of transition on the Zambian copperbelt. Parts 1 & 2. *Journal of Southern African Studies* 16(3):385–412; 16(4):603–21.

Fernandes, E. C. Manuel, and P. K. Ramachandran Nair. 1986. An evaluation of the structure and function of tropical homegardens. *Agricultural Systems* 21: 279–310.

Feschotte, Cedric, and Susan R. Wessler. 2001. Treasures in the attic: Rolling circle transposons discovered in eukaryotic genomes. *Proceedings of the National Academy of Sciences* 98:8923–24.

Fischer, Edward. 1999. Cultural logic and Maya identity. *Current Anthropology* 40:473–99.

Fowler, Cary, Geoffrey C. Hawtin, and Toby Hodgkin. 2000. Foreword to *Genes in the Field: On-Farm Conservation of Crop Diversity*, ed. Stephen B. Brush. Rome: International Development Research Centre and International Plant Genetic Resources Institute.

Fowler, Cary, and Pat Mooney. 1990. *Shattering: Food, Politics, and Loss of Genetic Diversity*. Tucson: University of Arizona Press.

Frank, Thomas. 2004. Lie down for America: How the Republican Party sows ruins on the Great Plains. *Harper's Magazine* 308:33–48.

Gallagher, Richard, and Tim Appenzeller. 1999. Beyond reductionism. *Science* 284: 79.

Game, Ann, and Andrew Metcalfe. 1996. *Passionate Sociology*. London: Sage.

Glick-Schiller, N. L. Basch, and C. Blanc-Szanton. 1992. *Toward a Transnational Perspective on Migration*. New York: New York Academy of Sciences.

Gonzales, Tirso A. 2000. The Cultures of the Seed in the Peruvian Andes. In *Genes in the Field: On-Farm Conservation of Crop Diversity*, ed. Stephen B. Brush, 193–216. Rome: International Development Research Centre and International Plant Genetic Resources Institute.

Goodwin, Brian. 1994. *How the Leopard Changed its Spots*. London: Weidenfield and Nicholson.

Gould, Stephen Jay, and Elisabeth S. Vrba. 1983. Exaptation—A missing term in the science of form. *Paleobiology* 8: 4–15.

Groves, Craig R., D. B. Jansens, L. L. Valutis, K. H. Redford, M. L. Shaffer, J. M Scott, J. V. Baumgartner, J. V. Higgins, M. W. Beck, and M. G. Anderson. 2002. Planning for biodiversity conservation: Putting conservation science into practice. *Bioscience* 52(6): 499–512.

Gupta, Akhil. 1998. *Postcolonial Developments: Agriculture in the Making of Modern India*. Durnharn and London: Duke University Press.

Haraway, Donna. 1988. Situated knowledge: The science question in feminism and the privilege of partial perspective. *Feminist Studies* 14(3): 575–99.

———. 1989. *Primate Visions: Gender, Race, and Nature in the World of Modern Science*. New York: Routledge.

Harlan, Jack R. 1972. Genetics of disaster. *Journal of Environmental Quality* 1: 12.

Hawkes, Jack. 1991. The importance of genetic resources in plant breeding. *Biological Journal of the Linnean Society* 43: 3–10.

Hayden, Cori. 2003. *When Nature Goes Public: The Making and Unmaking of Bioprospecting in Mexico*. Princeton and Oxford: Princeton University Press.

Helleiner, Jane. 1995. Gypsies, Celts and tinkers: Colonial antecedents of anti-traveller racism in Ireland. *Ethnic and Racial Studies* 18: 532–554.

Henke, Robert. 1997. The Italian mountebank and the *commedia dell'arte*. *Theatre Survey* 38: 1–30.

Heschel, Abraham J. 1965. *Who is Man?* Stanford, Calif.: Stanford University Press.

Hodgkin, Toby, A. H. D. Brown, Th. J. L. van Hintum, and E. A. V. Morales, eds. 1995. *Core Collections of Plant Genetic Resources.* Chichester, U.K.: John Wiley & Sons.

Hoffman, Michael P., H. David Thurston, and Margaret E. Smith. 1993. Breeding for resistance to insects and plant pathogens. In *Crop Improvement for Sustainable Agriculture*, ed. M. Brett Callaway and Charles A. Francis. Lincoln, Neb., and London: University of Nebraska.

Holden, John, James Peacock, and Trevor Williams. 1993. *Genes, Crops, and the Environment.* Cambridge and New York: Cambridge University Press.

hooks, bell. 1990. Talking back. In *Out There: Marginalization and Contemporary Cultures*, ed. R. Ferguson, M. Gever, T. T. Minh-ha, and C. West, 337–343. New York: The New Museum of Modern Art.

IRRI. 1993. *The IRRI Rice Almanac.* Los Banos, the Philippines: The International Rice Research Institute.

Itzigsohn, J. 1999. Immigration and the boundaries of citizenship: The institution of immigrants' political transnationalism. *International Migration Review* 34: 1126–54.

Jabs, Carolyn. 1984. *The Heirloom Gardener.* San Francisco: Sierra Club Books.

Jackson, Michael. 1995. Protecting the heritage of rice biodiversity. *Geojournal* 35(3): 267–74.

Jackson-Jones, Patricia. 1987. *When Roots Die: Endangered Traditions on the Sea Islands.* Athens and London: University of Georgia Press.

James, Alexander, K. J. Gaston, and A. Balmford. 2001. Can we afford to conserve biodiversity? *Bioscience* 51(1): 43–52.

Jarvis, Devra, and Toby Hodgkin. 2000. Farmer decision making and genetic diversity: Linking multidisciplinary research to implementation on-farm. In *Genes in the Field: On-Farm Conservation of Crop Diversity*, ed. Stephen B. Brush, 261–78. Rome: International Development Research Centre and International Plant Genetic Resources Institute.

Jarvis, Devra, Bhuwon Sthapit, Jose Luis Chavez, Mahamadou Sawadogo, Susan Bragdon, and Madhusudan Upadhyay. 2001. Strengthening the scientific basis of *in situ* conservation of agricultural biodiversity on-farm: IPGRI supported national partner case studies. Paper presented at *In-situ* Conservation of Agrobiodiversity, Lima, Peru.

Jiang, Ning, Zhirong Bao, Xiaoyu Zhang, Hirohiko Hirochika, Sean R. Eddy, Susan R. McCouch, and Susan R. Wessler. 2003. An active DNA transposon in rice. *Nature* 421: 163–72.

Johnson, Allen W. 1972. Individuality and experimentation in traditional agriculture. *Human Ecology* 1: 149–59.

Jonsson, Hjorleifur. 2001. Serious fun: Minority cultural dynamics and national integration in Thailand. *American Ethnologist* 28: 151–78.

Kamm-Gordon, W. J., C. L. Basczynski, W. B. Bruce, and D. T. Tomes. 1999.

Transgenic Cereals—*Zea mays* (maize). In *Molecular Improvement of Cereal Crops*, ed. I. K. Vasil. Dordrecht, Boston, and London: Kluwer Academic Publishers.

Kearney, M. 1995. The Local and the Global: The anthropology of globalization and transnationalism. *Annual Review of Anthropology* 24: 247–65.

Keller, Evelyn Fox. 1983. *Feeling for the Organism: The Life and Work of Barbara McClintock*. New York: W. H. Freeman and Company.

Khush, Gurdev. 1995. Modern varieties—Their real contribution to food supply and equity. *GeoJournal* 35 (3): 275–84.

———. 1996. Prospects and approaches to increasing the genetic yield potential of rice. In *Rice Research in Asia: Progress and Priorities*, ed. R. E. Evenson, R. W. Hjedt, and M. Houssain. London: CAB International in Association with the International Rice Research Institute.

Kikuchi, Kazuhiro, Kazuki Terauchi, Masamitsu Wada, and Hiro-Yuki Hirano. 2003. The plant MITE *mPing* is mobilized in another culture. *Nature* 421: 167–70.

Kloppenburg, Jack R. 1988. *First the Seed: Political Economy of Plant Biotechnology 1942–2000*. Cambridge: Cambridge University Press.

Koch, Christoff, and Gilles Laurent. 1999. Complexity and the nervous system. *Science* 284: 96–98.

Kropff, M.J., A. J. Haverkort, P. K. Aggarwal, and P. L. Kooman. 1995. Using systems approaches to design and evaluate ideotypes for specific environments. In *Eco-regional Approaches for Sustainable Land Use and Food Production*, ed. J. Bourma et al. Dordrecht: Kluwer Academic Publishers.

Lakoff, George, and Mark Johnson. 1980. *Metaphors We Live By*. Chicago: University of Chicago Press.

Lambek, Michael, and Paul Antze. 1996. Introduction: Forecasting memory. In *Tense Past: Cultural Essays in Trauma and Memory*, ed. Paul Antze and Michael Lambek, xi–xxxviii. New York and London: Routledge.

Lamont, Susan R., W. Hardy Eshbaugh, and Adolph M. Greenberg. 1999. Species composition diversity and use of homegardens among three Amazonian villages. *Economic Botany* 43: 312–26.

Latour, Bruno. 1993. *We Have Never Been Modern*. Cambridge, Mass.: Harvard University Press.

Lester, Julius. 1988. *More Tales of Uncle Remus: Further Adventures of Brer Rabbit, His Friends, Enemies, and Others*. New York: Dial Books.

Levitt, P. 2001. *Transnational Villagers*. Berkeley, Calif.: University of California Press.

Lipsitz, George. 1991. *Time Passages*. Minneapolis: University of Minnesota Press.

Livingstone, David N. 2003. *Putting Science in its Place: Geographies of Scientific Knowledge*. Chicago and London: The University of Chicago Press.

Lovejoy, Thomas E. 1997. Biodiversity: What is it? In *Biodiversity II*, ed. Marjorie L. Reaka-Kudla, Don E. Wilson, and Edward O. Wilson, 7–14. Washington, D.C.: Joseph Henry Press.

Manson, Steven M. 2001. Simplifying complexity: A review of complexity theory. *Geoforum* 32: 405–14.

Marcus, George E., and Michael M. J. Fischer. 1986. *Anthropology as Cultural Critique: An Experimental Moment in the Human Sciences*. Chicago: University of Chicago Press.

Maxted, Nigel, Brian Ford-Lloyd, and J. G. Hawkes. 1997. Complementary conservation strategies. In *Plant Genetic Conservation: The In Situ Approach*, ed. Nigel Maxted, Brian Ford-Lloyd, and J. G. Hawkes, 15–40. London: Chapman and Hall.

McClintock, Barbara. 1984. The significance of responses of the genome to challenge. *Science* 226: 792–801.

McDonald, John F. 1990. Macroevolution and retroviral elements. *BioScience* 4: 183–91.

McNamara, Brooks. 1995. *Step Right Up*. Jackson, Miss.: University Press of Mississippi.

Mignolo, Walter D. 2000. *Local Histories/Global Designs: Coloniality, Subaltern Knowledges and Border Thinking*. Princeton: Princeton University Press.

Milne, Bruce T. 1998. Motivation and benefits of complex systems approaches in ecology. *Ecosystems* 1: 449–56.

Mohanty, Chandra Talpade, and M. Jacqui Alexander. 1997. *Feminist Genealogies, Colonial Legacies, Democratic Futures*. London and New York: Routledge.

Moore, Barrington Jr. 1978. *Injustice: The Social Basis of Obedience and Revolt*. White Plains, N.Y.: M. E. Sharpe.

Myers, Norman. 1996. The biodiversity crisis and the future of evolution. *The Environmentalist* 16: 37–47.

Nabhan, Gary. 1989. *Enduring Seeds: Native American Agriculture and Wild Plant Conservation*. San Francisco: North Point Press. Reprint, Tucson: University of Arizona Press, 2002.

Nagel, C. R. 2002. Geopolitics by another name: Immigration and politics of assimilation. *Political Geography* 971–87.

National Academy of Sciences Report. 1972. *Genetic Vulnerability of Major Crops*. Washington, D.C.: National Academy of Sciences.

Nazarea, Virginia. 1998. *Cultural Memory and Biodiversity*. Tucson: University of Arizona Press.

———. 1999. A view from a point: Ethnoecology as situated knowledge. In *Ethnoecology: Situated Knowledge/Located Lives*, ed. Virginia D. Nazarea, 3–19. Tucson: University of Arizona Press.

Nazarea, Virginia, and Rafael Guitarra, comp. 2004. *Los Cuentos de Creación y Resistencia*. Quito, Ecuador: Abya-yala Press.

Nazarea, Virginia D., Robert E. Rhoades, E. Bontoyan, and G. Flora. 1998. Defining indicators which make sense to local people: Intracultural variation in perceptions of natural resources. *Human Organization* 52 (2): 159–70.

Nazarea, Virginia, M. Eleanor Tison, Maricel C. Piniero, Robert E. Rhoades. 1997. *Yesterday's Ways, Tomorrow's Treasures: Heirloom Plants and Memory Banking.* Dubuque, Iowa: Kendall/Hunt Publishing Company.

Nazarea-Sandoval, Virginia. 1995. *Local Knowledge and Agricultural Decision Making in the Philippines: Class, Gender, and Resistance.* Ithaca and London: Cornell University Press.

Nicolis, Gregoire, and Ilya Prigogine. 1977. *Self-Organization in Nonequilibrium Systems.* New York: John Wiley and Sons.

———. 1989. *Exploring Complexity.* New York: W. H. Freeman Company.

Norgaard, Richard B. 1988. The rise of the global exchange economy and the loss of biological diversity. In *Biodiveristy*, ed. E. O. Wilson, 206–11. Washington, D.C.: National Academy Press.

Odum, Eugene. 1971. *Fundamentals of Ecology.* Philadelphia: Saunders.

Orlove, Benjamin S., and Stephen B. Brush. 1996. Anthropology and the conservation of biodiversity. *Annual Review of Anthropology* 25: 329–52.

Ortner, Sherry. 1984. Theory in anthropology since the sixties. *Comparative Studies in Society and History* 26: 126–66.

———. 1995. Resistance and the problem of ethnographic refusal. *Comparative Studies in Society and History* 37: 173–93.

Ostrom, Eleanor, J. Burger, C. B. Field, R. B. Norgaard, and D. Policansky. 1999. Revisiting the commons: Local lessons, global challenges. *Science* 284: 278–82.

Padoch, Christine, and Wil de Jong. 1991. The house gardens of Santa Rosa: Diversity and variability in an Amazon agricultural system. *Economic Botany* 45: 166–75.

Patrick, Ruth. 1997. Biodiversity: Why is it important? In *Biodiversity II*, ed. Marjorie L. Reaka-Kudla, Don E. Wilson, and Edward O. Wilson, 15–24. Washington, D.C.: Joseph Henry Press.

Pauling, Linus, and Daisaku Ikeda. 1992. *Lifelong Quest for Peace: A Dialogue.* Boston: Jones & Bartlett Publishers, Inc.

Pimbert, Michel. 1994. The need for another research paradigm. *Seedling* 11: 20–32.

Piniero, Maricel Castillo. 2002. *Biodiversity and Marginality: Dilemma of Economic Development.* Ph.D. diss., University of Georgia, Athens.

Plucknett, Donald L., Nigel J. H. Smith, J. T. Williams, and N. Murthi Anishetty. 1987. *Gene Banks and the World's Food.* Princeton, N.J.: Princeton University Press.

Prance, G. T. 1997. The conservation of botanical diversity. In *Plant Genetic Conservation: The In Situ Approach*, ed. N. Maxted, B. V. Ford-Lloyd, and J. G. Hawkes, 3–14. London: Chapman and Hall.

Prigogine, Ilya. 1997. *The End of Certainty: Time, Chaos, and the New Laws of Nature.* New York: The Free Press.

Prigogine, Ilya, and Isabelle Stengers. 1984. *Order Out of Chaos: Man's New Dialogue with Nature.* Toronto: Bantam Books.

Proust, Marcel. 1934. *Remembrance of Things Past.* Trans. C. K. Scott Moncrieff and Andreas Mayor. New York: Random House.

RAFI (Rural Advancement Foundation International). 1997. *Human Nature: Agricultural Biodiversity and Farm-Based Food Security.* Canada: Rural Advancement Foundation International.

Rappaport, Joanne. 1990. *The Politics of Memory: Native Historical Interpretation in the Colombian Andes.* Cambridge, Mass.: Cambridge University Press.

Raven, Peter H., and Jeffrey A. McNeely. 1998. Biological extinction: Its scope and meaning for us. In *Protection of Global Biodiversity*, ed. Lakshman D. Guruswamy and Jeffrey A. McNeely, 13–32. Durham: Duke University Press.

Reddell, Rayford C. 1999. *Heirloom Roses.* San Francisco: Chronicle Books.

Rhoades, Robert E. 1974. The ecotone concept in ecology and anthropology. *Papers in Anthropology* 15: 23–26.

Rhoades, Robert E., and Anthony Bebbington. 1995. Farmers who experiment: An untapped resource for agricultural research and development. In *The cultural dimension of development: Indigenous knowledge systems*, ed. M. D. Warren, L. J. Slikkerveer, and D. Brokensha, 296–307. London: Immediate Technology Publications Ltd.

Rhoades, Robert E., and V. Nazarea. 1998. Local management of biodiversity in traditional ecosystems. In *Biodiversity in Agroecosystems*, ed. W. Collins and C. Qualset, 215–35. Boca Raton, New York, and London: ORC Press.

———. 2003. *Introduced Germplasm of Vietnam: Documentation, Acquisition, and Preservation.* Unpublished Report. Athens, Ga.: University of Georgia.

Rhoades, Robert E., Virginia Nazarea-Rhoades, and Maricel Piniero. 2001. Contrasting scientific and local valuations of land use change: The future visioning methodology. In *Bridging Human and Ecological Landscapes: Participatory Research and Sustainable Development in an Andean Agricultural Frontier*, ed. Robert E. Rhoades, 333–49. Dubuque, Iowa: Kendall/Hunt Publishing Company.

Ribiero, Gustavo L. 1997. Transnational virtual community? Exploring implications for culture, power, and language. *Organization* 4(4): 496–505.

Richards, Paul. 1986. *Coping with Hunger: Hazard and Experiment in a West African Farming System.* London: Allen and Unwin.

———. 1996. Culture and community values in the selection and maintenance of African rice. In *Valuing Local Knowledge: Indigenous People and Intellectual Property Rights*, ed. Stephen B. Brush and Doreen Stabinsky, 209–29. Washington, D.C.: Island Press.

Saldivar, David Jose. 1997. *Border Matters: Remapping American Cultural Studies.* Berkeley, Calif.: University of California Press.

Scott, James C. 1985. *Weapons of the Weak: Everyday Forms of Peasant Resistance.* New Haven and London: Yale University Press.

Seremetakis, C. Nadia. 1994. *The Senses Still: Perception and Memory as Material Culture in Modernity.* Chicago: University of Chicago Press.

Shiva, Vandana. 1989. *Staying Alive: Women, Ecology and Development*. London: Zed Books.
————. 1993. *Monocultures of the Mind: Perspectives on Biodiversity and Biotechnology*.
    London and Penang: Zed Books.
Smith, Eric Alden, and Mark Wishnie. 2000. Conservation and subsistence in small-
    scale societies. *Annual Review of Anthropology* 29: 493–524.
Soleri, Daniela, and David Cleveland. 1993. Hopi crop diversity and change. *Journal of
    Ethnobiology* 13: 203–31.
Soltis, Joseph, Rob Boyd, and Peter J. Richerson. 1995. Can group-functional behav-
    iors evolve by cultural group selection? An empirical test. *Current Anthropology* 36:
    473–83.
Soulé, Michael. 1993. Conservation: Tactics for a constant crisis. In *Perspectives on
    Biodiversity: Case Studies of Genetic Resource Conservation and Development*, ed. Chris-
    topher S. Potter, Joel I. Cohen, and Dianne Janczewski, 3–17. Washington, D.C.:
    American Association for the Advancement of Science.
Speaight, George. 1980. *A History of the Circus*. San Diego, Calif.: A. S. Barnes.
Steedly, Mary Margaret. 1993. *Hanging Without a Rope*. Princeton: Princeton Univer-
    sity Press.
Stewart, Kathleen. 1996. *A Space on the Side of the Road: Cultural Poetics in an "Other"
    America*. Princeton: Princeton University Press.
Stoddart, Helen. 2000. *Rings of Desire: Circus History and Representation*. Manchester,
    U.K.: Manchester University Press.
Stoler, Anne L. 1978. Garden use and household economy in rural Java. *Bulletin of
    Indonesian Economic Studies* 14(2): 85–100.
Stoller, Paul. 1995. *Embodying Colonial Memories: Spirit Possession, Power and the Hauka
    in West Africa*. New York and London: Routledge.
Streufert, Siegfried. 1997. Complexity: An integration of theories. *Journal of Applied
    Social Psychology* 27: 2068–95.
Strickland, Sue. 1998. *Heirloom Vegetables: A Home Gardener's Guide to Finding and Grow-
    ing Vegetables from the Past*. New York: Fireside Books.
Sutton, David E. 1998. *Memories Cast in Stone: The Relevance of the Past in Everyday Life*.
    Oxford, U.K.: Berg.
Swaminathan, M. S. 1982. Beyond IR36—Rice research strategies for the 80s. Paper
    presented at the International Centers' Week, World Bank, November 10. Wash-
    ington, D.C.
Takacs, David. 1996. *The Idea of Biodiversity: Philosophies of Paradise*. Baltimore, Md.:
    Johns Hopkins University Press.
Taussig, Michael. 1993. *Mimesis and Alterity*. New York: Routledge.
Thrift, Nigel. 1999. The place of complexity. *Theory, Culture & Society* 16: 31–69.
Tonkin, Elizabeth. 1992. *Narrating our Pasts: The Social Construction of Oral History*.
    Cambridge: Cambridge University Press.

Trouillot, Michel-Rolph. 1991. Anthropology and the savage slot. In *Recapturing Anthropology: Working in the Present*, ed. Richard G. Fox, 17–44. Santa Fe: School of American Research.

Tsing, Anna L. 1993. *In the Realm of the Diamond Queen: Marginality in an Out-of-the-way Place*. Princeton: Princeton University Press.

UNEP (United Nations Environmental Programme). 1994. Convention on Biological Diversity: Text and Annexes. UNEP/CBD/94/1. Geneva: The Interim Secretariat for the American Biological Diversity.

Upadhyay, M. P., and A. Subedi. 1999. Methods used to create a framework for implementation and management of in situ conservation on-farm in Nepal. In *A Scientific Basis for In Situ Conservation of Agrobiodiversity On-Farm: Nepal's Contribution to the Global Project* (Nepal Working Paper no. 1), ed. B. Sthapit, M. P. Upadhyay, and A. Subedi, 1–24. Rome: International Plant Genetic Resources Institute.

Urquia, Nuria. 2001. Constraints and opportunities for including *in situ* conservation within international and national genetic resources strategies. Workshop on *In situ* Conservation of Agrobiodiversity: Scientific and Institutional Experiences and Implications for National Policies, Lima, Peru.

Valladolid, Julio, and Frédérique Apffel-Marglin. 2001. Andean cosmovision and the nurturing of biodiversity. In *Interbeing of Cosmology and Community*, ed. John Grim, 639–70. Cambridge, Mass.: Harvard University Press.

van Noy, Rick. 2003. *Surveying the Interior: Literary Cartographers and the Sense of Place*. Reno and Las Vegas: University of Nebraska Press.

Vasavi, A. R. 1994. Hybrid times, hybrid people: Culture and agriculture in South India. *Man* 28: 283–300.

Vavilov, N. I. 1951. *The Origins, Immunity, and Breeding of Cultivated Crops: Selected Writings of N.I. Vavilov*. Trans. Chester K. Starr. New York: Rowland Press.

Vertovec, S., and R. Cohen. 1999. *Migration, Diasporas, and Transnaturalism*. Cheltenham: Edward Elgar.

Waldman, Amy. 2004. Indian soybean farmers join the global village. *New York Times*, Section A1. January 1.

Waldorp, Mitchell. 1992. *Complexity: The Emerging Science at the Edge of Order and Chaos*. New York: Simon and Schuster.

———. 1993. *Complexity*. New York: Viking.

Watson, James D. 1968. *Double Helix: A Personal Account of the Discovery of the Structure of DNA*. New York: Atheneum.

Weinberg, Steven. 1993. *Dreams of a Final Theory: The Search for the Fundamental Laws of Nature*. London: Vintage.

Weiner, Jonathan. 2000. *Time, Love, and Memory: A Great Biologist and His Journey from Genes to Behavior*. New York: Faber and Faber Limited.

Wessler, Susan. R. 1997. Transposable elements and the evolution of gene expression.

In *SEB Symposium, Control of Plant Development, Genes and Signs*, ed. A. Greenland, E. Meyerowitz, and M. Steer, 115–22.

———. 2001. Plant transposable elements. A hard act to follow. *Plant Physiology* 125: 149–51.

Wilcox, Bruce A. 1984. *In situ* conservation of genetic resources: Detriments of minimum area requirements. In *National Parks, Conservation, and Development*, ed. J. A. McNeely and K. R. Miller, 18–30. Washington, D.C.: Smithsonian Institution Press.

Wilkes, Garrison. 1991. *In situ* conservation of agricultural systems. In *Biodiversity, Culture, Conservation and Ecodevelopment*, ed. M. Oldfield and J. Alcorn, 86–101. Boulder, Colo.: Westview Press.

Wilson, Edward O. 1988. The Current State of Biological Diversity. In *Biodiveristy*, ed. E. O. Wilson, 3–18. Washington, D.C.: National Academy Press.

———. 1997. Introduction to *Biodiversity II*, ed. Marjorie L. Reaka-Kudla, Don E. Wilson, and Edward O. Wilson, 1–3. Washington, D.C.: Joseph Henry Press.

Withers, Mark A., and V. Meentemeyer. 1999. Concepts of scale in landscape ecology. In *Landscape Ecological Analysis*, ed. J. M. Klopatek and R. H. Gardner, 205–52. New York: Springer.

Wolf, Eric. 1982. *Europe and the People Without History*. Berkeley, Calif.: University of California Press.

Zerubavel, Yael. 1995. *Recovered Roots: Collective Memory and the Making of Israel National Tradition*. Chicago and London: University of Chicago Press.

Zhang, Qiang, John Arbuckle, and Susan R. Wessler. 2000. Recent, extensive, and preferential insertion of members of the miniature inverted-repeat transposable element family Heartbreaker into genic regions of maize. *Proceedings of the National Academy of Sciences* 97: 1160–65.

Zipes, Jack. 1988. Introduction: Toward a realization of anticipatory illumination. In *The Utopian Function of Art and Literature: Selected Essays*. Cambridge, Mass.: MIT Press.

Index

About the Author

• •

Virginia D. Nazarea is Professor of Anthropology and Director of the Ethnoecology/ Biodiversity Laboratory at the University of Georgia. Her research has focused on the situatedness of local knowledge and its distribution according to ethnicity, class, age, and gender. She has explored how this internal differentiation leads to a political ecology of cognition that on one hand shapes development trajectories and conservation strategies but on the other engenders its own forms of marginality and resistance. In biodiversity conservation, Nazarea has pursued related questions revolving around memory and countermemory at the cultural and individual level. Her publications include *Local Knowledge and Agricultural Decision Making: Class, Gender, and Resistance* (Cornell 1995), *Cultural Memory and Biodiversity* (University of Arizona Press 1998), and *Ethnoecology: Situated Knowledge/Located Lives* (University of Arizona Press 1999). She has also published memory banking protocols in English and Spanish.